PRESERVING PORCHES

The evolution of the front porch is a microcosm of the decline of community. In the half-century before World War II verandas were simply de rigueur. They were places for observing the world, for meeting friends, for talking, for knitting, for shelling peas, for courting, and for half a hundred other human activities. The front porch was the physical expression of neighborliness and community. With a much-used front porch, one could live on Andy Hardy's street, where doors need not be locked, where everyone was like a family, and where the iceman would forever make deliveries. With a front porch, one could live in Brigadoon, Shangri-La, and Camelot, all in one.

KENNETH T. JACKSON, *CRABGRASS FRONTIER*

PRESERVING PORCHES

RENEE KAHN AND **ELLEN MEAGHER**

AN OWL BOOK   HENRY HOLT AND COMPANY   NEW YORK

Published by Henry Holt and Company, Inc.,
115 West 18th Street, New York, New York 10011.
Published in Canada by Fitzhenry & Whiteside Limited,
195 Allstate Parkway, Markham, Ontario L3R 4T8.

Library of Congress Cataloging-in-Publication Data
Kahn, Renee.
Preserving porches / Renee Kahn and Ellen Meagher.—1st ed.
    p.   cm.
"An Owl book."
Includes bibliographical references.
ISBN 0-8050-1209-5
1. Porches—United States—Conservation and restoration.
I. Meagher, Ellen.   II. Title.
NA8375.K34   1990
728'.028'80973—dc20   90-4012
                                                       CIP

Henry Holt books are available at special discounts
for bulk purchases for sales promotions, premiums,
fund-raising, or educational use. Special editions
or book excerpts can also be created to specification.

For details contact:
Special Sales Director
Henry Holt and Company, Inc.
115 West 18th Street
New York, New York 10011

First Edition

Designed by Kate Nichols

Printed in the United States of America
Recognizing the importance of preserving the written word,
Henry Holt and Company, Inc., by policy, prints all of
its first editions on acid-free paper. ∞

Portions of this book were published previously as a handbook
available from the Historic Neighborhood Preservation Program, Inc.

10 9 8 7 6 5 4 3 2 1

To the memory of the late Alan Burnham,
noted architectural historian and founder of
the American Architectural Archive

Contents

PART TWO

Authors' Note

For over a decade, the Historic Neighborhood Preservation Program, Inc., has served as consultant to the Stamford Community Development Program, a federally funded housing rehabilitation agency. As preservationists, our role was to ensure that the historic character of Stamford's inner city was maintained, and to encourage neighborhood pride as an antidote to urban blight.

We soon realized that a lot of our work centered on the repair or reconstruction of porches. Open to wind, snow, and rain, porches are among the most vulnerable elements of an older house. The problem is intensified by poverty, which leads to hard use and lack of maintenance. We also realized that well-maintained porches gave a clear signal of neighborhood well-being, while rotting or badly remodeled porches sent off an equally strong message of disinvestment and neglect.

Although most of the damage we encountered was rooted in lack of money, well-intentioned nonprofit housing rehabilitation programs were as guilty as low-income homeowners or absentee landlords of shoddy or inappropriate porch repair. Modern safety and fire codes also helped disfigure porches, requiring alterations that violated the historic appearance of the porch. Even when the owner wanted to do the "right thing," he or she had difficulty finding out what that "right thing" was.

In response, the Historic Neighborhood Preservation Program churned out endless drawings of porches and porch details. We trained carpenters. We explained how to use epoxy to repair rotted porch posts, and counseled contractors on sources for replica posts and rails. In 1984, we applied for and received funding from both the Stamford Community Development

Program and the Connecticut Historical Commission to prepare a handbook on porch repair. The initial printing of two hundred copies was sent to local preservation groups and quickly disappeared. Recipients soon complained of having had their copies borrowed and not returned. As requests for books came in from as far away as Texas and Alabama, we realized that the need for a guide to preserving porches was not only statewide but nationwide. After all, National Trust for Historical Preservation statistics showed that there were *sixteen million dwellings* in the United States built prior to *1930*. Given our experience in the field, we could safely estimate that at least *fifteen million* of those had porches in need of repair.

This present edition of *Preserving Porches* is approximately three times the size of the original handbook. While still concentrating on nineteenth-century examples, we have expanded our range to include Colonial and twentieth-century houses and examples from around the country. Regional variations certainly exist, but the wide distribution of builders' pattern books during the nineteenth century, as well as improvements in mass production and distribution, tended to give a certain sameness to architecture in the United States. In order to be useful to the greatest number of people, we concentrated on typical, everyday porches, though we couldn't resist throwing in a few spectacular, one-of-a-kind examples.

Preserving Porches is meant to be a practical book, designed for homeowners, architects, handymen, and carpenters. Everyone will read the book for different reasons: the carpenter will look for practical pointers, the architect might further his knowledge of porch history and design, while the homeowner will be better able to understand and evaluate what needs to be done.

We know, however, that many people will read the book for no other reason than simple love of the subject. Porches seem to embody everyone's fond memories of the past: visits to Grandma, summer nights, the house we knew as children. Porches evoke much that was wonderful and is now lost. Perhaps by preserving them we can recapture some of the values they have come to represent.

PRESERVING PORCHES

Introduction:
The Rise and Fall of the American Porch

Porches are as synonymous with American culture as apple pie. While not unknown in Colonial times, they rose to nationwide popularity in the decades before the Civil War, and remained in fashion for almost one hundred years. Ironically, the very social and technological forces that made them both popular and possible were eventually responsible for their decline.

The term "porch" is derived from the Latin word *porticus*, or the Greek word *portico*, both of which signify the columned entry to a Classical temple. During the Middle Ages, "porch" was used to describe a covered vestibule to a cathedral where worshippers could gather to socialize before or after the service. The romantic Victorians preferred more pretentious words such as "veranda" (with or without an *h* on the end), "piazza," or "loggia" to the modest-sounding "porch." They used the words more or less interchangeably; "veranda," however, tended to connote a larger porch of West Indian origin, while "loggia" usually signified an arched gallery set into the main body of the house. "Portico" was reserved for the columned and pedimented entryways of the Classical Revival buildings. Until the last quarter of the nineteenth century, the word "porch" itself most often described a small, enclosed vestibule or covered rear entrance, and did not acquire its present meaning and widespread use until after 1875. "Piazza" was a favorite word for "porch" in the Charleston area; "gallery" or "galerie" was popular in the Gulf states; while "stoop," taken from the Dutch word *stoep*, was used nationwide to describe a stepped-up entry to the house. The term "umbrage," meaning "shade," even appears occasionally, although it's just another term for "porch." Recent studies by the American Dialect Society indicate regional preferences rather than any major stylistic rationale for the word used to describe a porch.

1

Figure 1. A c. 1250 B.C. wall painting from an Egyptian tomb depicts a comfortable country villa with a columned porch overlooking the garden.

The original concept of a porch can be traced back to the overhanging rock shelters of prehistoric times. One can also safely assume that most folk-houses in warmer climates contained some sort of shading that both cooled the interior and protected the exterior walls (Fig. 1). Ancient Greek and Roman dwellings placed columned verandas as shaded walkways around an interior garden. In Italy during the Middle Ages and Renaissance, arcaded loggias, open on one side, were occasionally set within the body of a public building, such as a hospital, to provide a shaded outdoor space. In fact, the word "piazza," meaning "plaza," may have been derived from the arcaded ground-floor walkways along the Piazza San Marco in Venice.

In northern Europe, however, true porches were rarely if ever seen, and American porches seem to have been derived from other primary sources.

Although no examples survive, there is some documentary evidence derived from old prints and drawings that porch shelters appeared rather early in Colonial times. They made their first significant appearance after 1730. One theory is that they were brought here by Dutch-Anglo traders who observed the verandaed plantation houses of the Caribbean islands. Porches were most popular in the southern colonies, where they provided relief from the sultry climate. In eighteenth-century New England, however, porches appeared occasionally on inns and taverns, or along waterways where the Caribbean trade had an impact.

Different climatic conditions, combined with the architectural tradition they brought from home, encouraged French, Spanish, English, and even Dutch settlements to develop distinctive kinds of porches. With the exception of a few taverns and inns, however, the typical Colonial house in New England found little need for anything but an entry porch until well into the 1840s.

But why did porches proliferate after 1840, and why did they vanish less than a century later? As is so often the case, economic, technological, and social forces lay behind what seemed to be an aesthetic decision. The front porch owed much of its newfound popularity to an increase in free time, the result of industrialization and massive population growth. The authors of the many, widely read builders' pattern books of the mid-nineteenth century were well aware of the importance of leisure, usually reserving porches for better houses and omitting them from humble farmhouses or workers' cottages. Why provide a porch for someone who could neither afford to build it nor had the time to enjoy it? For the first time in American history, there was a substantial leisure class, free from the endless survival chores of the Colonial era.

Vast numbers of immigrant workers provided domestic labor, while improvements in heating, lighting, and cooking equipment further eased the homeowner's burden. Technological advances in the cutting of lumber

Figure 2. Nineteenth-century improvements in power-saw equipment made it possible to construct an elaborate front, back, or side porch. Complex posts, rails, and brackets could be ordered through catalogs or copied by any moderately competent carpenter from pattern book designs.

and the mass production of nails allowed a lone carpenter and his helper to quickly erect complex structures. The new framing technique that made this possible was called a "balloon frame," a lightweight network of sticks that replaced the heavy timber frame of Colonial times.

Industrialization not only created a middle class with increased wealth and leisure; it made possible a degree of ornament previously unavailable to all but the very rich. Elaborate columns, brackets, and cornice details, once laboriously carved by hand, were now mass produced. Prefabricated lengths of cast or wrought iron replaced the time-consuming blacksmith's art, with highly ornate posts, rails, and fences now literally turned out by the mile at a fraction of their former cost (see Fig. 16). Complicated porch shapes, once expensive and difficult to construct, could be quickly assembled with machine-made parts (Fig. 2). Decorative details were now

Figure 3. This Queen Anne—style residence in Orange, New Jersey, designed by H. Hudson Holly, was at one time the home of the inventor Thomas Alva Edison. The house's impressive size and complexity clearly indicated the economic success and high social status of its owners.

available to all, with a network of new railroads and canals to bring them practically to the homeowner's front door.

While the Industrial Revolution made elaborate porches technically possible, it also set off an Arcadian counter-movement that made them psychologically attractive. It is not surprising that the widespread adoption of porches appeared at the same time as the Hudson River School in painting, and the Transcendentalist movement in religion and literature. Nineteenth-century landscape painters looked upon the grandeur of our new nation with pride, and agonized over the disfiguring encroachment and pollution of industry. The Transcendentalists, including Thoreau and Emerson, held a romantic view of nature that emphasized the unity of man, nature, and God. Andrew Jackson Downing, a landscape architect and horticulturalist, set down this philosophy in a series of influential architectural pattern books that exhorted the public to escape from the increasingly unpleasant urban scene by building "Country Houses," taken from the title of his most popular book, *The Architecture of Country Houses* (1850). What better place to commune with nature than from the scenic veranda of a sylvan home? Although the narrow porches of the Downing era did not lend themselves as much to social interaction as later versions, they did provide a means of integrating the house with its natural sur-roundings.

H. Hudson Holly, a successor to Downing, devoted another widely read pattern book to what he called "Country Seats," places where the nouveau-riche industrialist and his family could escape the "unwhole-someness" of city life. Even the title of the book was meant to conjure up images of the English gentry on their magnificently landscaped estates (Fig. 3).

By the end of the Civil War all restraint was set aside and porches became a dazzling display of technological virtuosity. Even modest cottages displayed ornamental porches with boxed or turned posts and cut-work rails. By the 1880s, improvements in mechanized wood turning enabled the public to indulge in the look of medieval "turnings" at a price every budget could afford. Turned posts, rails, and lintels became the rage. On the whole, except for the most northern states such as Maine, where every drop of sunlight was to be conserved, the porch now became a universally accepted feature of the American house. Once a response to difficult climatic conditions in hot and humid sections of the country, the porch found a broader purpose and more widespread use.

Until World War I, porches remained a social and architectural necessity, along with those other accoutrements of a slower pace of life: wicker furniture, rocking chairs, and the porch swing (Fig. 4). By the mid-1800s, the front porch had become an informal parlor, a trellised, open-air window for the hothouse Victorian world. Toward the end of the century, central heating and electric lights eliminated the need to restrict porches to a position and size that would not block out the sun. Porches became deeper and darker, often further shaded by awnings, screens, and foundation plantings. After World War I, the conventional front or wrap-around porch was gradually replaced by rear or side porches.

Aside from the practical difficulties of maintenance, why did porches fall out of favor with the American public? Interestingly enough, much of the blame can be placed on the automobile. The front porch was no longer an idyllic setting where one could relax and commune with nature. Exhaust fumes and the noise of a steady stream of cars and trucks had rendered it inhospitable and unhealthy. The street became devoid of passersby and neighborly interaction, and sitting on the porch lost much of its appeal. The automobile-dependent suburbs were built up with imitation Tudor, Spanish, and Colonial houses, all of which had no front porch. Sometimes there were side or rear porches, or even second-story sleeping porches, but the traditional across-the-front "sitting" porch was on its way out. The lovers who had traditionally "spooned" on the porch swing were now miles away, in the backseat of the family car.

Although front, back, and side porches were all eventually replaced by the back patio, the patio too was soon abandoned for the comfort of a playroom, den, or bedroom with air-conditioning and a TV set. Porches, no longer considered useful indoor/outdoor spaces, were enclosed or lopped off. Where one once could see the flicker of gaslight or hear friendly chatter into the night, there is now the faint colored glow of the TV screen and the steady hum of the air conditioner. The wonderful American porch, a product of modern technology and inventiveness was, ironically, also its victim.

After many years of houses being built without front porches, there

Figure 4. When William McKinley ran for president of the United States in 1896, he conducted a "front porch campaign" designed to endear him to the American public. Note the parlorlike decor of Mc-Kinley's porch, with its elaborate wicker furniture, patterned carpet, and potted palms.

Figure 5. The Sward House in Seaside, Florida, designed in 1985 by Deborah Berke, a New York architect, features a two-story porch. The screened, lower portion allows for interaction with passersby, while the upper one provides ocean views and cooling breezes.

Figure 6. **This** New Yorker *cartoon illustrates the all-too human need for familiar surroundings. (Drawing by Bernard Schoenbaum, © 1987 by The New Yorker Magazine, Inc.)*

has been a recent trend to include them as a selling point in a new house. Of course, in many cases, it's just "window dressing," a vestigial appendage never intended to be actually used. In planned communities such as Seaside in northern Florida, however, there is an attempt to re-create the social interaction and human scale of the nineteenth-century small town (Fig. 5). Buildings here are *required* to have porches, and they are seen as integral to the developer's goal of "a streetscape that is familiar, friendly, southern and traditional."

Perhaps we have learned something of value in the past few decades and by "preserving porches" we will preserve something very special about our nation and ourselves (Fig. 6).

> The porch promotes grace and comfort. It promotes good conversation simply by virtue of the fact that on a porch there is no need for it. . . . It is our reviewing platform and observation deck, our rostrum and dais, the parapet of our stockade, the bridge of our ship.
>
> —Garrison Keillor, *We Are Still Married*

PART ONE

1

Colonial Architecture

Seventeenth-century houses in the northern colonies were largely based on the medieval building traditions the early settlers had brought from England. Modest in concept and relatively devoid of ornament, they were asymmetrical in plan, with steep gabled roofs, small diamond-paned windows, and second-story overhangs. Although building documents of the period refer to "porches," they were not what we think of as porches today, but rather enclosed two-story entry bays attached to the front of the house (Fig. 7).

In the South, few examples of seventeenth-century architecture remain, and most of these have been substantially altered over the years. To the best of our current knowledge, they were one-story brick structures with steeply gabled roofs and large chimney stacks at either end. Houses made of wood were probably quite common as well but have not survived into modern times, and there is little evidence as to the kind of porches, if any, they had (Fig. 8).

Georgian Architecture, 1730–1820

By the 1730s, the influence of English architecture under the reign of the "Georges" reached America. Based on the designs of the sixteenth-century Italian Renaissance architect Andrea Palladio, Georgian forms reflected the increasing affluence and sophistication of the colonists. These up-to-date fashions from London were brought to the New World by a number of widely read builders' handbooks known as "pattern books," which explained to the local housewright how to construct fashionable doorways, windows, cornices, and interior trim.

Figure 7. The projecting, gabled entryway of the Pynchon Mansion, a seventeenth-century house that once stood in Springfield, Massachusetts, was referred to at the time as a "porch," a term derived from the covered entrance to an English medieval church.

9

Figure 8. The upper right-hand corner of this early seventeenth-century engraving of an Indian massacre may inadvertently provide us with our first view of a New World porch. Note the heavy timber-frame construction and the way the porch is placed under the main roofline—a common feature of Caribbean and French Colonial architecture.

Figure 9. An Ionic-columned and pedimented entry porch provides a note of Palladian grandeur to an otherwise modest Federal-era house in New Haven, Connecticut.

In keeping with Classical ideals, houses became more symmetrical in plan, now emphasizing horizontal lines and balance. Rooflines were still quite steep, although the narrow medieval gable had all but disappeared. Gabled and gambrelled roofs were most popular in the North, while tall, hipped roofs were more commonly seen in southern architecture. Wood was still the material of choice in the North, brick in the South. Windows became larger and more plentiful, surmounted by molded pediments derived from Renaissance architecture.

Ornament was most heavily used around the entrance to the house (Fig. 9). Doors were paneled, with flat, molded columns known as pilasters on either side. The pediment over the door received most of the decorative attention, coming in a number of shapes: arched, triangular, complete or broken at top or bottom, and with a variety of molded trim. In the North, entry porches occasionally consisted of simple, gabled overhangs resting on pairs of Classical columns.

Porches also seem to have made an early appearance on taverns and inns—possibly because these were places of leisure for both travelers and town residents. In a book called *Weld Travels* (published in 1795), the author reported on his trip from Philadelphia to Baltimore: "Every ten miles up on this road there are taverns which are all built out of wood and much in the same style, with a porch in front the entire length of the house."

Given the sultry climate of much of the South, it is not surprising that the first extensive use of porches occurred there, especially in and around

the city of Charleston, South Carolina. By the mid-1700s, a "marriage" appears to have taken place between the formal porticoes of Palladian architecture and the cooling, breeze-filled verandas of Caribbean or African origin. One of the first and finest examples of a Georgian porch can be found at Drayton Hall (1738–1742) outside of Charleston (Fig. 10). Drayton Hall features a two-story, recessed porch inspired by one of Palladio's original designs (Fig. 11).

In 1787, George Washington attached the famous, two-story, full-height piazza to his house at Mount Vernon. It was not added to the front, as might be expected, but to the rear façade, which overlooked the Potomac River (Fig. 12). Washington's design was influenced by one of the most popular pattern books of the period, Batty Langley's *The City and Country Builder's and Workman's Treasury of Designs.* The square columns of the piazza were made possible by America's vast supply of massive timbers.

Even after the Revolution, Georgian forms continued to dominate American architecture. The Adam style (1780–1820), a lighter, more delicate version of Georgian, influenced building throughout the country, especially in the fast-growing, prosperous cities of the eastern seaboard. High-style Adamesque, also known as Federal style, houses are still to be found in great numbers from Portland, Maine, to Savannah, Georgia (Fig. 13).

Basically Georgian in plan, "Adam" (named after the Adam brothers,

Figure 10. The two-story, recessed, Palladian porch at Drayton Hall was one of the first of its kind in the colonies. It demonstrated the sophistication of its owner while providing a practical response to the heat and humidity of a Charleston summer.

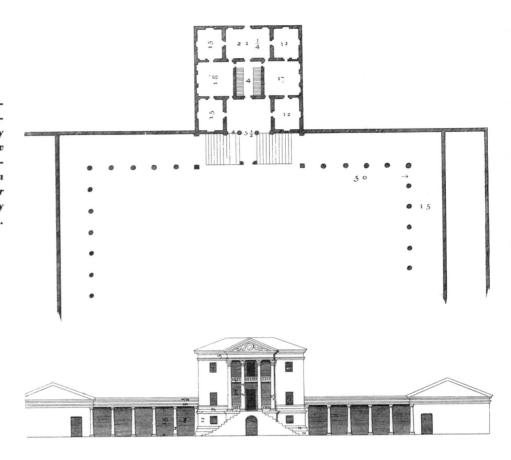

Figure 11. Palladio's sixteenth-century Italian villas adapted remarkably well to eighteenth-century American plantation living. The New World aristocracy often found themselves drawing upon Palladian sources for their porticoed manor houses, flanked on either side by smaller, utilitarian dependencies.

Figure 12. In 1787, George Washington attached one of the earliest full-height, full-width piazzas in the colonies to his house at Mount Vernon. Although monumentally scaled, it provided an informal outdoor living area for Washington's family, where they could take afternoon tea while enjoying a view of the Potomac.

Figure 13. Boscobel, built in 1808 in Garrison, New York, by wealthy merchant States Dyckman, reflects the fashionable ideas he acquired during his many business trips to England. The delicately columned and detailed two-story porch was an unusual feature in the North, although fairly common by then in sophisticated southern coastal cities.

fashionable English architects) incorporated newly discovered Roman or Pompeiian elements such as urns, swags, and garlands. The ubiquitous eagle ornament, however, was a purely American contribution. Elaborate entryways featured elliptical fanlights and delicately divided sidelights, along with oval-shaped or Palladian windows. Exquisitely proportioned entry porches now began to appear. Rectangular or semicircular in shape, they often displayed elegantly balustraded rooflines and rested on Doric or Ionic columns with Classical entablatures and dentilled friezes.

In the South, the Palladian-inspired entry porch became increasingly popular. Unlike Drayton Hall, with its recessed porches, one- or two-story, classically columned porticoes were now added to the façade of a building, forming a separate entry bay. These porches most frequently consisted of a heavy, pedimented gable resting on Roman Doric columns, although there were any number of idiosyncratic or regional variations. Second-story "sitting" balconies were placed behind the two-story, full-height version, a characteristic that became increasingly popular in Greek Revival architecture in the South prior to the Civil War.

Between 1790 and 1830, a handful of Roman Revival houses were constructed under the influence of gentleman-architects such as Thomas Jefferson. The style was used primarily for public buildings, where it seemed appropriate for a new republic. In the few Roman Revival residential buildings, the columned entry porch or portico achieved grand proportions, featuring anywhere from two to eight or even ten columns in an impressive Classical colonnade. By the 1830s, however, Greek Revival forms replaced the Roman model and reached a far wider audience.

Figure 14. Despite its humble materials and simple construction, this c. 1833 slave house on a plantation in Watsonia, Alabama, managed to provide a porch, as well as a "dog trot" breezeway between the two main rooms of the house.

Although we tend to associate southern architecture with impressive plantation and town houses, a good percentage of the population lived in modest folk-houses with little or no architectural pretension. Porches seemed to have appeared quite early, perhaps as a result of African building traditions brought over by slaves. From the little evidence that remains, it seems that full-width, shed-roofed porches may have been attached to one-room-deep dwellings by the late eighteenth century (Fig. 14). Another vernacular version, perhaps also of slave origin, was the so-called dog-trot house. Here, the two halves of the house were separated by a covered passageway open at front and back, with access to the rooms on either side. This internal porch, the first breezeway in America, was a shaded area where household chores could be performed supposedly while the family dogs trotted back and forth. As in the better houses of the South, climate was a major factor in determining architectural form.

The French Colonial House, 1700–1830

Despite the vast French empire in North America, only a few hundred examples of French Colonial architecture remain. Most of these can be found in Louisiana, Mississippi, or Missouri. The typical Louisiana Territory rural cottage was derived from a number of different sources. Its steeply pitched, hipped roof resembles the moisture-shedding thatched roofs of Medieval Norman architecture, a feature that may have been introduced to French colonies in America by way of French settlements in Canada. These "pavilion" roofs, as they were known, were extended

Figure 15. The difficult climate of the Louisiana delta region encouraged the development of broad verandas known as galleries. Raised high above the damp ground, these porches also served as an exterior hall, with doors leading to the main downstairs rooms. Homeplace in St. Charles Parish, Louisiana, is typical of the French plantation-style house with its origins in Caribbean, French Norman, and Neo-Classical architecture.

out on all four sides of the house to create wide porches known as galleries, closely resembling those of the typical West Indian plantation house of the time. Breeze-filled galleries rested on foundations of brick, or stucco-covered wood, and provided direct outdoor access for the rooms of the house. The wide overhang of the porch also served to protect the fragile stucco-over-half-timber exterior walls. The elevation of the main floor appears to have come from Caribbean sources, but may just as well have been a practical response to similar climatic conditions (Fig. 15).

Porch posts were simple wooden sticks originally sunk directly into the ground, although few examples have survived the effects of insects and moisture. By the beginning of the nineteenth century, however, Classical columns became popular, giving the galleried porch something of the look of a Greek or Roman temple grafted onto a house with a steep, medieval roof.

The best surviving examples of French Colonial urban architecture are found in New Orleans. Despite the fires that destroyed a good deal of the city in the late 1700s, there are still a handful of typical side-gabled or hipped-roof cottages with sheltering overhangs facing the street. By the 1830s, improvements in manufacturing led to the creation of the elaborate cast-iron porches on the upper stories that have come to typify southern cities, especially New Orleans (Fig. 16). Cheaper than the older, handmade wrought or cast iron, and more durable than wood in a hot and humid climate, cast iron soon changed the look of French Colonial urban architecture. Interestingly, these products of American technology gave French New Orleans a distinctive look almost never seen in France itself.

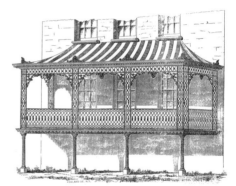

Figure 16. By the 1830s, improvements in the mass production of cast and wrought iron encouraged their use throughout the country. Florid details such as these were popular in the cities of the South, especially New Orleans, where they proved more practical in a humid climate than conventional wood ornament. Metal porches, roofs, balconies, and fences could be shipped in sections from the factory, and easily bolted together on-site.

The Spanish Colonial House, 1700–1850

During the eighteenth century, the Spanish developed a far-flung empire on North American soil, exerting control over an area ranging from Florida on the East Coast to San Francisco on the West. As in other forms of Colonial architecture, European prototypes were modified by local building traditions and climate.

The houses of the Spanish colonies are distinguished by their thick masonry walls of adobe brick or stuccoed stone. The few, small, window openings originally lacked glass and were protected from the heat by solid wood shutters. The most familiar building type had a low-pitched, gabled roof covered by interlocking red clay tile. Less common was the flat-roofed version with massive horizontal timbers supporting a heavy earth or mortar roof.

Porches were most frequently placed overhanging the ground floor, where they served their customary function in warm climates of shading the downstairs rooms and providing a cool, outdoor space for chores (Fig. 17). As in traditional Spanish architecture, on the rear of the house there were also long, narrow porches called "corredors" that opened onto an internal courtyard and functioned as sheltered passages between rooms with no connecting interior doors.

As Anglo influence increased during the nineteenth century, different kinds of porches began to appear on the façades of buildings built by the descendants of Spanish colonists. These could be created by extending the roof overhang forward to create a covered area. Another version, the

Figure 17. Modest but functional, the cantilevered balcony-porch of the Old Whaling Station in Monterey, California, exemplified a popular southwestern approach to cooling and shading the front of a Spanish Colonial house.

Figure 18. The flared eave of a gambrel-roofed Dutch Colonial house such as the Dyckman House in New York City could be brought forward to provide a porchlike overhang to shelter the front wall of the house. Columns were often added at a later date to reflect the fashion for Classical architectural forms.

second-story balcony-type porch, was cantilevered out over the front of the building. Porch posts were usually plain, heavy timbers, often with massive curvilinear brackets. Later porch posts take on the attributes of the Greek Revival and Italianate styles popular elsewhere in the country during the mid-nineteenth century.

The Dutch Colonial, 1625–1820

Dutch Colonial architecture is an amalgam of many influences that have little or no provable relationship to the native architecture of Holland. The earliest surviving rural Dutch houses are generally made of stone or brick, with later examples in clapboard or shingle. Much controversy exists as to the origin of the characteristic gambrelled roof and the flared overhanging eaves, both of which became popular after 1750. The gambrel roof, considered typically Dutch, was probably English in origin and in widespread use throughout the English colonies as well. The spring eave is a more puzzling element, perhaps an adaptation of the Flemish-French tradition of extending the thatched roof out in a gentle curve to protect fragile plaster walls underneath from the elements. It is this spring eave extension of the roof that gradually evolved into a nineteenth-century sitting porch, with simple, square supporting posts probably added at a later date (Fig. 18).

2

Greek Revival,
1830–1855

The first truly romantic movement to sweep the country was the Greek Revival. Classical architecture, filtered through the Renaissance eyes of Palladio, had influenced American building for almost one hundred years, but it was not until the late 1700s that an attempt was made to go back to original Greek and Roman sources. While gentlemen-architects such as Thomas Jefferson encouraged a Roman Revival, it never acquired widespread popularity. As Russell Lynes cleverly put it, "The excursion which had paused briefly in Rome and borrowed a few ideas there, seemed to have fallen upon Greece and plundered it."

The enthusiasm for all things Greek had both political and archaeological origins. Although discoveries in the eighteenth century had familiarized the public with Pompeiian and Roman architecture, it was not until several volumes of measured drawings of the Acropolis were published in the early 1800s that the "Greek Mania," as it was called, took hold. Politically, the Greek War of Independence from the Turks (1821–1830) struck a sympathetic, nationalistic chord, and by 1850, America was covered by pseudo-Greek temples (Fig. 19). One visitor from England remarked that all the buildings he saw looked like Greek temples, from "the privies in the back to the State House."

Although there were few trained architects and not a single school of architecture in the country, dozens of widely circulated pattern books guided the local builder. Especially popular were Asher Benjamin's *The American Builder's Companion* (1827) and Minard Lafever's *The Modern Builder's Guide* (1833). Decorative elements could be copied from these books or purchased ready-made. A rather freewheeling, mix-and-match attitude developed among builders, creating many idiosyncratic interpretations of what was meant to be a rigid Classical format.

Although we tend to think of Greek Revival houses as gabled temples surrounded by full-height colonnades, they came in different sizes, shapes, and regional variations. While the residential version of the Parthenon was the *sine qua non* of the style, most Greek Revival houses were traditional rectangular boxes with applied Classical touches. The Greek Revival style had its most lasting impact on the plantation houses of the South, where grand porticoes could be easily grafted onto the already entrenched French plantation house with its broad, shaded galleries.

Although the style was displaced in the more sophisticated urban centers by the Gothic and Italianate Revivals of the late 1840s and 1850s, it persisted in the South and in rural interior states until the Civil War. A farmhouse variant with its pedimented gable facing front continued to be built until the 1930s.

In its simplest form, a Classical pediment could be suggested by outlining the triangular shape of the gable with heavy, projecting moldings. The easiest way to make the house look like a real temple, however, was to turn the narrow end of the house around to face the street, and pull the gable out six to eight feet, resting it on a row of Greek columns. By judicious application of molding plus a few authentic details such as bands of fretwork or triglyphs and metopes, a modest vernacular box metamorphosed into the latest fashion. Molding could be used to create pilasters, flattened columns at either corner of the façade. Doors and windows were simple and rectilinear, surrounded by heavy, molded trim. The entryways are often identified by the plain horizontal and vertical lines of the transom and sidelights, in contrast to the fussy divided lights and arched transoms of the preceding Federal era.

Although real Greek temples were made of marble, Americans were forced to settle for wood. The effect of masonry, however, could be created by using flush board instead of clapboard on the front of the house, and carving or painting it to look like blocks of stone.

In general, Greek Revival porches have a grandeur that differentiates them from the informal, indoor-outdoor sitting areas of later houses. We refer to them as porticoes, not porches, columned entryways designed to impress the visitor with the high cultural achievements of the house's occupants. In many cases, older Colonial buildings were made fashionable

PATTERN BOOKS

Although native and European building traditions certainly had an impact on American architecture, most builders acquired their ideas from pattern books. These varied from the works of the sixteenth-century Venetian architect Andrea Palladio and other high-style European imports to carpenters' handbooks illustrating ways to tack on a bit of fashionable detail to a vernacular gabled box.

The gentlemen-builders of the colonial South, however, modeled their homes mostly after the designs of two Englishmen, Christopher Wren and James Gibbs. Gibbs's *A Book of Architecture* (1728) was the most important book in the colonies during the last half of the eighteenth century. While his work was aimed at the more scholarly builder, there were also numerous carpenters' handbooks. Especially popular was Batty Langley's *The City and Country Builder's and Workman's Treasury of Designs*, which appeared in 1740 and was reprinted in eleven editions up to 1808.

The first successful pattern book published in America was Asher Benjamin's (*The Country Builder's Assistant*, 1797). A host of others followed, including works by Minard Lafever, a self-taught architect. *The Young Builder's General Instructor* appeared in 1829, *The Modern Builder's Guide* in 1833, and *The Beauties of Modern*

Architecture in 1835. Lafever's designs had a profound influence on early-nineteenth-century architecture in New York City.

By the 1840s, American pattern books turned from Renaissance influences to the Greek Revival, and later looked to Gothic and Italian villa forms for inspiration. Andrew Jackson Downing published a series of influential treatises on rural houses, their construction, conveniences, and even furniture. His two most successful books, *Cottage Residences* (1842) and *The Architecture of Country Houses* (1850), went through numerous editions, many of them published after his death in 1852. Downing promoted an Arcadian, rural version of the Gothic style, although his handsomely illustrated books also included picturesque Italian villas and some highly conjectural Swiss chalets.

The post–Civil War building boom encouraged a new generation of pattern books. Gervase Wheeler, Calvert Vaux, H. Hudson Holly, A. J. Bicknell, and George Woodward were especially successful and prolific, publishing thousands of copies in numerous editions. The architects Palliser and Palliser produced twelve titles from 1876 through 1883, while A. J. Bicknell and Co. turned out at least ten new books from 1870 to 1886. William T. Comstock and his son published the magazine *Architecture and Building* from 1882

to 1932, chronicling a vast panoply of eclectic styles. These widely distributed builders' guides created a certain nationwide uniformity in architectural design. With minor variations, you could see the same buildings from one end of the United States to the other.

The twentieth century saw little diminution of the importance of pattern books. In 1901, Gustav Stickley began publication of the monthly journal known as *The Craftsman*, which promulgated an American version of William Morris and the English Arts and Crafts style. Stickley reproduced views of houses that epitomized his philosophy and offered architectural plans and construction drawings for a small membership fee. He also strongly influenced the development of the bungalow, a one-story version of the Craftsman style that soon became America's most popular small house. A flood of bungalow pattern books emanated from California prior to World War I, some even offering precut packages of lumber to be assembled by local labor.

Pattern books remain in wide use today. Magazine counters everywhere often contain a half-dozen publications displaying multiple visions of the American Dream. Whether a Cape Cod cottage, reproduction saltbox, or an ersatz hacienda, a few dollars will still bring you the house of your choice, by return mail.

Figure 20. The Greek temples adapted unexpectedly well to both the southern climate and temperament, intermingling in this case with English Colonial and French Creole architecture. The eight colossal Tuscan columns of The Shadows-on-the-Teche (1831–1834), in New Iberia, Louisiana, managed to reach their full two-story height by resting on high, un-Classical pedestals.

Figure 21. The traditional, gable-roofed "box" could be given architectural importance by the judicious application of a few "Classical" elements. In the case of the former Orrville Academy in Orrville, Alabama, a pedimented portico juts out unexpectedly from the center of the long side of the house. The pair of handsome fluted Ionic columns are flanked by square, paneled posts—less expensive than columns but equally impressive. A row of dentil molding under the cornice, and paneled, corner pilasters complete the transformation of this modest, clapboard house.

by the addition of a Greek portico, thereby creating some interesting architectural hybrids (see Chapter 13).

Although the most sought-after version of a residential portico had a pediment and a row of columns across the façade, many American homeowners settled for far less, often just a modest entry porch with a small gabled pediment resting on a pair of Ionic or Doric columns. The columns, however, were what mattered most: Greek Revival patterns books were quite specific as to what was acceptable form. Oliver Smith in his 1854 *The Domestic Architect* states that the height of a Doric column—the most commonly used Greek "order"—should be nine times its diameter, but ten times if Ionic, and if Corinthian, twelve (Fig. 20). Fluted columns were historically accurate, but expensive. Inexpensive, but *totally* inauthentic, "boxed" columns (see Fig. 20) were cased in wood boards ornamented with molded panels, bases, and capitals (Fig. 21).

Figure 22. The William Rodman House in New Bedford, Massachusetts, is distinguished by its incongruous application of a lavish, Corinthian colonnade onto a rough, stone "box." Although the columns rest on a Classical, stepped platform, the absence of a triangular pediment gives the house a somewhat unfinished look.

Figure 23. The Classical origin of the columns is echoed by the exquisite row of cast-iron "lyres" that form the balcony rail of the G. G. Thompson House in Tuskegee, Alabama.

Over the row of columns you needed a full entablature consisting of an architrave (the lintel), a frieze (plain or ornamented), and an overhanging cornice. A triangular pediment was desirable but optional. Pattern books clearly showed the local carpenter how to build these Classical forms, although many details were now mass produced and available through catalogs. As conventional one-story "sitting porches" became popular later in the period, they were attached—without pediment—to the front or side of the house. A row of Greek columns, however, served the function of porch posts.

Although some versions of the Greek Revival house rest on a high foundation, most are no more than three or four steps above the ground. Slabs of stone were often used as steps, although in some cases wooden stairs run the full width of the portico, enhancing the desirable "Parthenon" effect (Fig. 22).

Porch railings were rarely used, as they interfered with the attempt to replicate a Classical colonnade. Most of the rails we see today on Greek Revival houses are later additions. In the South, however, a second-story sitting porch was often set behind the colonnade, and these balconies frequently featured elaborate cast-iron railings of considerable grace (Fig. 23).

Gothic Revival, 1840–1860, 1880

As interest in the rigid Greek Revival format waned, the more picturesque Gothic and Italianate Revivals took over. Gothic Revival was patterned loosely after fifteenth-century English medieval architecture and revived in England in the mid-1700s. The style was popularized in America by Alexander Jackson Davis, one of the nation's first architects, and by his friend Andrew Jackson Downing, a noted horticulturalist and landscape architect. Despite Davis's and Downing's enthusiastic support, Gothic Revival never achieved the popularity of contemporaneous Greek Revival or Italianate styles.

Most American examples of Gothic Revival were built between 1840 and 1860, although a later, polychromed masonry version known as Victorian Gothic lingered on until the 1880s (Fig. 24). Primarily designed to blend with the natural landscape, it did not lend itself well to urban dwellings on narrow city lots.

Gothic Revival architecture was characterized by steeply pitched roofs with cross gables and wall dormers. It also featured pointed arches and paired windows, as well as elaborately carved foliate trim around porch and gables. It was this profusion of delicate tracery known as "gingerbread" that distinguished Gothic Revival more than anything else (Figs. 25, 26).

While Downing encouraged the use of masonry, as an "authentic" Gothic material, he was aware of the American preference for wood. If masonry was unavailable or unaffordable, then a vertical siding known as "board and batten" would have to suffice. These elaborate wood interpretations of masonry style became known as Carpenter Gothic, and their popularity far exceeded that of the stone or brick originals.

Figure 24. A somber, multicolored masonry version of Gothic Revival known as Victorian Gothic appeared soon after the Civil War. This picturesque rectory in Stamford, Connecticut, was designed by H. Hudson Holly, an influential pattern book architect of the latter half of the nineteenth century.

Figures 25, 26. The ornamental band that ran along the edge of the gables came in almost as many variations as the houses themselves. Some resembled pendant icicles, others had a foliage quality, as if the vines of the garden had come to entwine the entire house.

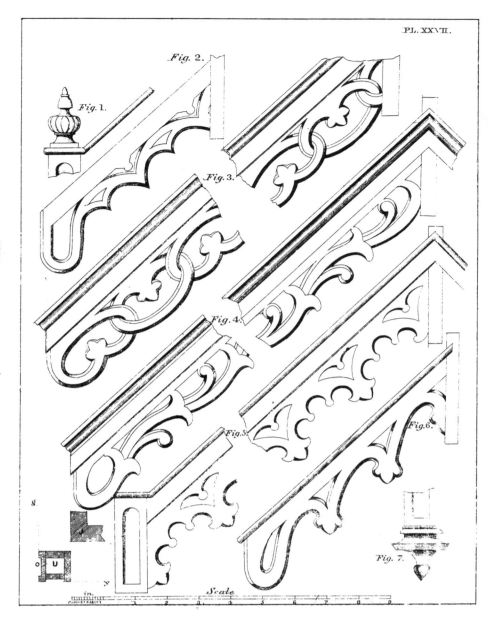

Given the period's enthusiasm for nature, it is not surprising that the "sitting" porch became an integral part of the Gothic house. It was a way to bridge the gap between the built and the natural environment (Fig. 27). Gothic Revival porches came in many different sizes and orientations. While the most popular version went across the front of the house, other plans called for side, corner, or rear porches. Their use and position depended upon sun or shade requirements at different times of the day or year. Although the main gable of the house was steeply pitched, the porch roof usually appeared flat, even though it was slightly hipped to allow for drainage and covered with seamed sheets of painted metal. In early versions, entry porches sometimes had a balcony with an elaborate pierced-work rail placed on top of the porch roof. The underside of the

porch roof often did not have a ceiling, but left the structural elements exposed (Fig. 28).

When it came to porch ornament, the builder of a Gothic Revival house had considerable latitude. New, machine-cut ornament could be "mixed and matched." Free adaptations of Gothic motifs, such as three-lobed trefoils or four-lobed quatrefoils, added an authentic note (Fig. 29).

Porch posts varied from boxed posts, with beveled corners cut at a 45-degree angle, to hexagonal casings, or clusters of thin, round colonettes designed to suggest the compound columns of the fifteenth-century Gothic cathedral. Another popular though totally unmedieval version, was the trellis-type post. These varied from plain lattice panels placed between two wooden uprights to complex foliate carvings made out of wood or cast iron. A third type was created out of flat boards with Gothic-inspired cutout designs (Fig. 30).

In the early phases of the period, a Gothic cresting made of wood often crowned the front edge of the porch roof. In post–Civil War examples, elaborate valance panels were placed between the capitals of the columns and the porch lintel. Again, the pierced designs reflected the influence of Gothic tracery (Fig. 31).

Figure 27. The porch of a Gothic Revival house served as an outdoor parlor, connecting the house to its (one hoped) idyllic surroundings. Painters and writers of the period encouraged this Arcadian attitude at the same time as industrial expansion blighted more and more of the American landscape.

Figure 28. This extended porch at Lyndhurst, in Tarrytown, New York, one of the earliest Gothic Revival houses in America, is reminiscent of the aisle or ambulatory of a Gothic church, with its exposed roof structure.

Figure 29. A typical Colonial house could be easily "Gothicized" by the addition of wood gingerbread derived from the ornamental stone framework of medieval stained-glass windows. The porch of this otherwise modest house in New Haven, Connecticut (below), is enlivened by three- and four-holed cutouts on the brackets and lintel panel (opposite at top), designed to suggest Gothic trefoils and quatrefoils.

Figure 30. *Porch posts came in many versions; most were available through lum-*
beryard catalogs or easily constructed by a carpenter. A cluster of slender colo-
nettes was the most authentically Gothic-looking, but trellis-type posts with cutout
designs were also acceptable.

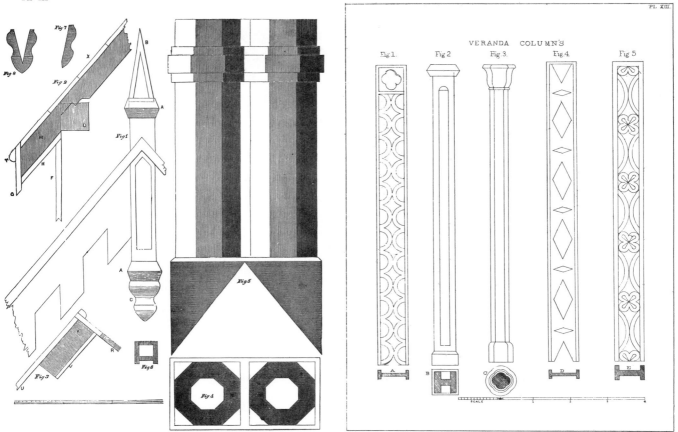

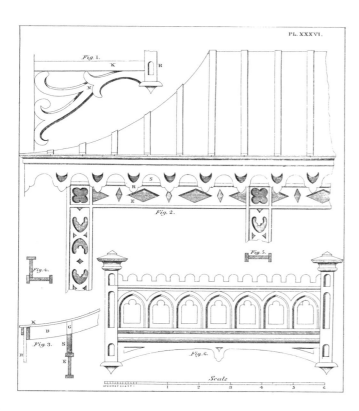

Figure 31 (above left). Floral and geometric cutouts were used to create complex plays of light and shadow on the façade of the Gothic Revival house. Elaborate porch valances, brackets, and roof cresting were relatively inexpensive ways to suggest medieval origins.

Figure 32 (above right). By the 1860s, the American appetite for ornament appeared almost insatiable, as illustrated in the fanciful combination of Gothic and Italianate influences in this Cape May, New Jersey, cottage.

Porch brackets, also ran the full gamut, from simple, arched sticks that created the effect of an arcade to elaborate curvilinear brackets with floral or Gothic motifs. Small paired brackets, anywhere from six to ten inches high, were placed under the cornice of the porch roof, decorating the otherwise plain frieze board between the porch columns and the roof.

While many Gothic Revival houses were built without any porch rails, pattern books such as Calvert Vaux's *Villas and Cottages*, published in 1857, suggest a number of different possibilities. These varied from simple one-and-a-half-inch stick rails to more elaborate, cutwork patterns (Fig. 32).

Porch aprons were created by cutwork or lattice panels that allowed the underside of the porch to be ventilated while screening unsightly debris from view. Porch stairs were now made primarily of wood instead of stone, and stair rails, if any, continued the pattern of the main porch rail.

4

Italianate,
1840–1885

Following the route of previous architectural fashions, the Italian Villa style came to America by way of England. Loosely based on the picturesque palazzos and villas of sixteenth-century Italy, it soon surpassed Greek and Gothic Revival in popularity. Between 1850 and 1870, the Italian Villa style captured the romantic imagination of the American public, particularly in the Northeast and the rapidly expanding towns and cities of the Midwest. The style dominated American architecture until the financial crisis of the 1870s put a temporary halt to construction. When building activity resumed several years later, public taste had passed on to the newer Queen Anne and Romanesque styles. Italianate influences lasted longest and strongest in resort architecture, reaching its most ornate form in shorefront communities such as Cape May, New Jersey, and Martha's Vineyard (Fig. 33).

Also called "Tuscan Revival," its varied examples are distinguished by low-pitched, hipped or gabled roofs with wide, bracketed eaves. These elaborate cornice brackets visually defined the style, causing the writer Edith Wharton to refer to examples as "Hudson River Bracketed."

In its most popular format, the house was a square or rectangular box topped by a central cupola or "belvedere," an Italian word meaning "beautiful view" (Fig. 34). From these rooftop vantage points inhabitants could commune with their supposedly idyllic surroundings.

Another common plan was L-shaped, with a three-story square tower loosely based on the Italian "campanile," or bell tower, in the corner of the L. Other versions included a central tower at the intersection of a T-shaped plan (Fig. 35).

In addition to towers, brackets, and low-pitched roofs, Italianate

Figure 33. The Italian Villa style, with its broad, arcaded verandas, was well suited to resort architecture. The Chalfonte, Cape May, New Jersey's oldest hotel, made visitors feel as if they were strolling along the Piazza San Marco in Venice, instead of being only a day or so away from home.

Figure 34. One of the most popular interpretations of an Italian villa was the box-shaped house with its rooftop observatory known as a "cupola," or a "belvedere." Not only did the observatory provide a pleasant vista, but it also served as an exhaust system, allowing unhealthy vapors from primitive plumbing and heating equipment to escape from the house.

houses were distinguished by round arched windows, often in narrow pairs; they can be found in the gable of the most modest vernacular houses, even those with little or no other distinguishing architectural detail. Elaborate window hoods and pediments are seen in the grander versions of the style, an expression of its underlying Italian Renaissance origin. In general, the overall quality of the Italian Villa is a pleasing balance of Classical forms in a picturesque composition.

In later, more elaborate versions, the portion of the porch in front of the main entrance to the house was accentuated by a slightly projecting pedimented portico, a refinement derived from original Renaissance villas. Many Italianate houses also display Gothic characteristics, as it was common for both house builders and pattern book designs to rather freely mix elements from both styles (Fig. 36).

Just as in contemporary Gothic Revival houses, almost every Italianate house had at least one porch. It wasn't called a porch, however, but a piazza, a veranda, or a loggia, terms that indicated the high cultural pretensions of the houses and their occupants. Often nine feet deep, expansive and airy, these single-story verandas increased in decorative intensity until reaching the height of extravagance around the time of the Civil War.

The siting of the porch varied according to the overall orientation of the house and the location of its most scenic views. Small, bracketed entry coverings sufficed for urban houses, but the rural or suburban Italian Villa had everything from full front porches to partial front porches, L-shaped porches, or even small side porches tucked into the corners of the house. Loggias, arched passageways set within the main body of the house,

also became popular, especially in pre–Civil War versions of the style. Another version had a balustraded balcony set on top of a small, flat-roofed entry porch. Porch roofs were usually shallow-hipped with structural elements visible from underneath, although wood-slat ceilings start to appear at this time.

As for the porch roofs themselves, builders' pattern books suggested either painted metal or canvas with painted stripes in imitation of canvas awnings (Fig. 37).

A dozen or more different kinds of porch posts and columns were used, ranging from simple boxed versions with beveled corners cut at a 45-degree angle, to elaborate interpretations of Doric, Ionic, or Corinthian columns. The boxed column, usually six to eight inches square, was embellished by narrow strips of molding at the top and bottom meant to suggest a Classical capital and base. Its wooden sides were left plain or paneled to add architectural interest. Posts of all kinds were placed on rail-height pedestals articulated by paneling and other applied ornament (Fig. 38). Although single, evenly spaced columns were the most typical format, twin or tripled columns placed at the corners or bordering the entrance were also to be found. Ornate, trellis-type posts were often identical to those found on Gothic Revival houses of the period. These were usually made of wood, although machine-made cast-iron and wrought-iron sections, easily bolted together, were increasingly available. The

Figure 35 (above left). Masonry was the preferred "authentic" material for Italian Villas; however, in most communities, only the wealthy could afford it. The Morse-Libby House in Portland, Maine, now a museum, features a good number of Renaissance architectural elements, including corner quoins, stone balustrades, window pediments, and, best of all, a three-story "bell" tower modeled after the Italian campanile.

Figure 36 (above right). Among the more exotic interpretations of the Italian Villa style in America are the Captain Doullut Houses in New Orleans. Although twentieth century in origin, this pair of houses built by a former riverboat captain manages to combine the jigsaw ornament found on Mississippi steamboats with Creole and Japanese elements.

Figure 37 (right). Riddell's Architectural Designs, published in 1861, advocated painting tin porch roofs, especially when the roof was visible from the street. Since Italian Villas were supposed to be painted in soft, "stone" colors—beiges, grays, pale yellows, and creams—the awning-striped roofs could serve as an accent, perhaps candy pastels or contrasting colors.

Figure 38 (below left and center). "Boxed" posts, constructed out of flat boards with mitered corners, could be lavishly trimmed with panels and molding. Curved brackets were used to give a simple post-and-lintel porch the look of an arcade, while a row of toothlike dentils under the cornice further emphasized Classical origins.

Figure 39 (below right). Mass-produced cast-iron elements could be assembled on-site to create a wide variety of elaborate porch ornament. The former St. James Hotel, later a warehouse in Selma, Alabama, reflects the extravagant forms possible in this practical, yet relatively inexpensive, material.

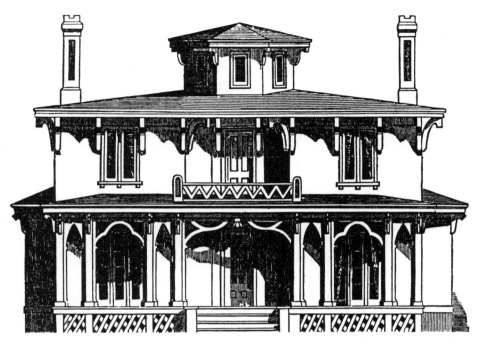

Figure 40. *Building a true arch required the use of masonry; however, curved wooden sticks were an easier way to achieve a similar effect. These curvilinear porch brackets echo the brackets of the roofline with its cupola observatory.*

Figure 42. *At least a half-dozen separately ordered items were assembled to create the porch columns, cornice, and lintel of this Italianate house in Milford, Connecticut. The most original effect, however, was achieved by applying sections of ordinary half-round molding on the columns to give the effect of a Classical capital.*

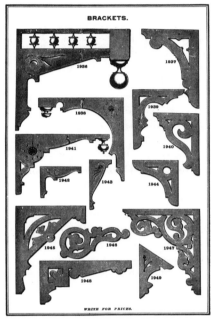

Figure 41. *This page from the Universal Molding Book,* published by W. L. Churchill, *displays the wide variety of readily available ornament that could be ordered through a catalog.*

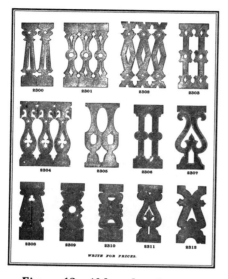

Figure 43. *Although quite easy to make by hand, many kinds of porch rails were commercially available. The chief attraction of these cutwork designs lies in the intricate dark and light patterns the holes form when placed next to one another in a row.*

complex, curlicued designs resembled the tendril patterns of Victorian script (Fig. 39).

Porch brackets also came in many different variations, often with arched sticks and panels that created the effect of an arcade (Fig. 40). In post–Civil War interpretations of the Italianate, brackets became increasingly heavy and complex, sometimes created by sandwiching several one-inch boards together and recessing the even-numbered ones to create interesting shadows. Floral designs, either cut out or incised, adorned the sides of the brackets (Fig. 41). Smaller rows of brackets rested under the porch cornice, visually separating the sections of an elaborate frieze (Fig. 42).

In this pre–building code era, many Italianate porches were built without any railings at all. When present, railings ranged from simple one-and-a-half-inch-square sticks to one-by-four-inch boards with cutout designs, or elaborate urnlike turned balusters, or even highly complex pierced patterns (Fig. 43). In any case, railings were quite low by modern standards, often no more than twenty-eight inches high and aligned with the tops of the post pedestals (see Figs. 33, 34, 35, 38).

While many Italianate porches were built close to the ground, others were raised on platforms several steps high. As in the Gothic Revival style, the porch apron consisted of diagonal or square lattice, or flat boards with intricate, pierced designs. Unfortunately, many examples of ornamental aprons have deteriorated over the years and have been replaced by simple lattice panels.

5

Stick Style,
1850–1885

One of the few distinctively American nineteenth-century styles, Stick is primarily a wood interpretation of masonry Victorian Gothic. Although popular in the builders' pattern books of the 1860s and 1870s, few high-style Stick houses were ever actually built. The best examples are seen in the coastal resort towns of the Northeast and in California. Stylistically, it bridged the gap between the Gothic and the Queen Anne, with some Swiss chalet elements tossed in for good measure (Fig. 44).

Influenced by A. J. Downing's insistence on "truthfulness" in architecture, and the writings of the English architect Charles Locke Eastlake (the author of *Hints on Household Taste*, 1868), the Stick house was characterized by its applied (but *un*truthful) exterior wood framing. This arrangement of horizontal, vertical, and diagonal boards was purely surface decoration and bore little, if any, relationship to the actual balloon-frame structure underneath. Varied patterns of clapboard and shingles were placed in the spaces created by the stickwork.

Picturesque and asymmetrical, Stick-style houses were dominated by their steeply pitched, gabled roofs with distinctive stickwork peak ornaments, and broad, overhanging eaves. Strong diagonal or slightly curved braces were inserted in several places on the exteriors, supporting everything from the angle of the gable to the roofs of the wraparound verandas (Fig. 45).

Although few structures were built, Stick influences carried over into the highly textured Queen Anne–style house of the last quarter of the century, where even modest, vernacular cottages had an applied skeleton of flat boards nailed down between bands of clapboard and shingle siding. In many cases, Queen Anne and Stick style intermingled to such a degree

Figure 44. America's ample supply of wood encouraged its use both inside and outside the house. This Stick-style residence, which still stands along the Connecticut shore, is a fanciful interpretation of medieval European folk architecture. Stick-style houses were praised for their structural "honesty," although in reality most of the "exposed structure" was nothing more than applied ornament.

Figure 45 (opposite, at top). Most frequently found in seaside resort areas, Stick-style dwellings often featured porches on all three stories. These precarious-looking overhangs, perhaps derived from the balcony-porches of Swiss chalets, provided ocean breezes along with an attractive view.

that it is often difficult to characterize the house as being one style or the other. Unfortunately, the modern tendency to re-side Victorian houses makes it even harder to tell them apart.

Stick-style houses feature broad and spacious verandas, often wrapped around more than one side of the house. Since many examples were built in seashore vacation areas, wide porches were functional as well as decorative. Second- or even third-story covered porches were also popular, and bedrooms opened directly onto the porch. It was these upper-story porches set under broad overhanging eaves that gave Stick its resemblance to a Swiss chalet (see Fig. 45).

Figure 46. The Benedict Miller House in Waterbury, Connecticut, now occupied by the University of Connecticut, is distinguished by the striking arrangement of horizontal and vertical sticks that form the porch rails. The monotony of an unbroken row of railing is avoided by using turned newel posts at intervals to suggest Gothic finials and pendants, and by criss-crossing the center rails to form an X.

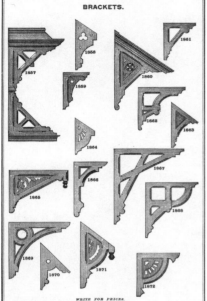

Figure 47 (above left). Angled braces with beveled edges gave a "structurally honest" look to porch and gable brackets in the Stick-style house.

Figure 48 (above right). King-post trusses imitated the massive, timber ceilings of the English Gothic church. They were used to accent the gabled entry to the porch, as well as on the main gables of the house.

Porch posts were striking, generously constructed of solid pieces of wood, sometimes eight to ten inches square, with later versions resembling sausage casings.

Porch balustrades were often quite intricate arrangements of one-inch or larger sticks (Fig. 46). Chinese-type lattice grills or interlocking squares or X's were popular, as were sausage-shaped turned spindles or Swiss chalet–style boards with cutout patterns. Porch aprons also displayed cutout boards or lattice panels to both decorate and ventilate the underside of the porch. Heavy, chamfered wood angle brackets replaced ornate curvilinear ones, forming a Y-shape with the porch posts (Fig. 47). These were meant to be structurally "honest" and expressive of medieval building traditions. Turned, king-post trusses with diagonal cross-pieces were popular in porch entry gables, as well as on the main gables of the house (Fig. 48). Post-1875 versions of both Stick and Queen Anne used carved stickwork sunbursts and sunflowers to ornament the porch pediments, motifs taken from the fashionable English Arts and Crafts movement of the period (see Fig. 68).

6

Second Empire,
1855–1885

The Second Empire style, with its characteristic "French" roof, became popular during the decade prior to the Civil War. Unlike previous Greek, Gothic, and Italianate Revivals, which looked to the past for inspiration, Second Empire was based on America's admiration for contemporary French culture under the reign of Napoleon III (1852–1870), the so-called Second Empire. One of the outstanding achievements of Napoleon's rule was the expansion of the Louvre, which brought back the double-pitched mansard roof developed in the seventeenth century by the French architect François Mansart (Fig. 49). The Second Empire style dominated American house construction from 1860 to 1880, when it was gradually supplanted by a new English import, the Queen Anne.

Except for the distinctive roof, Second Empire houses closely resembled Italian Villas in basic plan and ornament, although mansard roofs were also grafted onto Gothic, Italianate, or Stick-style structures (Figs. 50, 51).

The mansard roof came in many different variations: straight, concave, convex, even double or S-curved (Fig. 52). Straight and concave versions were most common with multicolored slate or metal shingles on the steep lower hip of the roof and galvanized sheet metal on the flatter top section. Sometimes the entire roof was covered with a metal such as galvanized zinc. One company, the Philadelphia Iron Works, advertised that it could make entire "French roofs," dormers and all, in fireproof metal and deliver them to the site ready to install. Ornate cast-iron cresting anywhere from one to two feet high was attached to the top ridge of the roof, hiding the shallow, flat portion from view. As in the Italian Villa style, cupolas were often placed at the high point of the roof, visually crowning the composition. The lower portion of the roof was pierced by multiple dormers

Figure 49. The closest that most fashionable Americans came to owning a chateau was to place a French mansard roof on their house. Not only did the double-pitched roof have high cultural connotations, but it provided considerably more usable headroom in the attic than the traditional gable or hip roof.

39

Figure 50. While many houses of the period had a certain purity and consistency of design, others borrowed freely from a variety of unrelated, co-existing styles. The steep medieval tower and the heavy Stick-style porch of the Frederick Miller House (1888) in Stamford, Connecticut, bear little architectural relationship to the pedimented gables or curvilinear brackets.

Figure 51. Blocklike and symmetrical, Second Empire houses often retained the popular center tower of the Italianate style, but with a steep mansard instead of a flat, low-hipped roof.

surmounted by the Renaissance-derived hoods or pediments seen elsewhere on the windows and doors of the house. The overhanging cornice rested on brackets that were similar in shape to those of the Italianate style, although both cornice and brackets never became as large or important as they did in Italian villas. The formal balance and symmetry of the Second Empire house was accentuated by heavy moldings and details such as string courses or corner quoins. Entry doors were often arched pairs with etched-glass upper panels. French doors or windows faced out onto the porch, adding a further note of elegance.

The decorative elements of the Second Empire porch generally followed Italianate sources. Every house had at least one porch, except for urban row houses, where a bracketed hood or small, columned entry porch sufficed (Fig. 53). Porches were placed across the entire front or back, or wrapped around the corner in an L-shaped plan. The most popular porch support was a boxed or solid wood post, anywhere from six to eight inches thick, with beveled edges, a type also commonly found on Italianate houses of the period (Fig. 56). More elaborate, post—Civil War porches featured paired or tripled posts set on paneled pedestal bases. Less expensive houses made do with simple molding at the top and bottom of plain wooden sticks.

Bracket styles varied widely, generally following Italianate or one of the other stylistic influences popular during the 1860s and 1870s (Fig. 57). Tendril-like designs were incised or cut out of the sides of the bracket. Lintel panels were sometimes placed under the cornice and ornamented with pierced, Gothic-style openings that were also used on the porch

Figure 53. The main entrance of a town house such as the John Anderson House on Orange Street in New Haven, Connecticut, was usually accentuated by a small entry portico. Few porch columns accurately followed Classical orders, and, as shown here, often bear only passing resemblance to Doric, Ionic, or Corinthian prototypes.

HOTELS AND RESORTS

Throughout most of American history, hotels and lodging houses have been distinguished by elaborate verandas. Some of the earliest known porches in the colonies were found on eighteenth-century inns and taverns, perhaps influenced by the galleried "coaching" inns of Elizabethan England. Whether urban or rural, an extravagant expanse of porch often signaled the presence of a place to rest from the rigors of travel. In town, a multistoried porch provided not only an economical exterior passageway, but a vantage point from which to view the life of the main street.

During the first half of the nineteenth century, the veranda expressed the broad, pantheistic attitudes of the Transcendentalist thinking of the day.

The concept of a veranda appealed to the life-styles of the burgeoning new middle class and its desire to "connect" with the rapidly deteriorating American landscape. Similar feelings were expressed by the Hudson River School of American painters, whose popularity paralleled the rise of the great resort hotels. By the 1830s, a network of railroad, canals, bridges, and improved roads enabled travelers to reach scenic areas previously inaccessible or too far from home for a casual getaway.

The veranda of a resort hotel was its most distinguished architectural feature. Lavish colonnaded walkways, often two to three stories high, dom-

inated the monumental resort hotels of the early nineteenth century. A c.1830 view of the piazza of Congress Hall in Saratoga Springs, New York, displays a two-story Tuscan colonnade, its pillars entwined with vines to give the appearance of a certifiable "Classical" ruin (Fig. 54).

Hotels built in the Greek Revival or Italian Villa style characterized the pre–Civil War era, while Mansard, Stick, and Shingle styles dominated the latter half of the century. In rural areas, verandas were sited to take advantage of the best scenic view, and while usually placed on only one side of the building, there are many examples of the wraparound variety.

Figure 54. The social aspect of hotel porches is evident in this 1830s view of guests promenading on the piazza of the Congress Hall Hotel in Saratoga Springs, New York. Matchmaking and gossiping were as important a part of resort life as looking at scenery.

Multistoried verandas provided guests with their own personal access to an often spectacular view (Fig. 55). It mattered little if the bedroom was small and cramped when the vacationer was only a few steps from the whole outdoors. Elaborate cutwork rails or turned balustrades provided a protective barrier between the nature lover and the often precipitous view. No expense was spared to create lavish decorative detail. Ornamental brackets, posts, and rails were all characteristic of resort architecture in the nineteenth century.

While magnificent views and healthy summer breezes justified long hours on the veranda, these lofty sentiments may merely have been an excuse for the people-watching, the courting, and the gossiping that gave the nineteenth-century resort porch its dominant flavor and purpose.

The size of the hotel veranda soon became a source of discussion and status. Hotels often advertised the length or square footage of their verandas as a means of enticing guests. Henry James in *Portraits of Places* describes the Grand Union Hotel in Saratoga as having the largest piazza in the world. A savvy vacationer knew that in inclement weather a certain number of laps around the veranda would substitute for his morning constitutional.

By the twentieth century, the veranda was tamed and removed from its intimacy with the landscape. Screened porches were glassed in, and, later, air-conditioned to prevent contact with insects and inclement weather. Veranda space contracted, as open areas were enclosed to provide additional rooms or parlor-corridors. While rattan furniture and plants still preserved the indoor-outdoor feeling, furniture was arranged to provide for social interaction rather than mountain views. Just as the rear patio supplanted the front porch in residential architecture, the poolside deck has become the hotel veranda's modern equivalent. Verandas, where they exist at all today, generally take the form of a series of balconies for individual rooms or covered corridors.

Figure 55. In this 1907 photograph, guests are shown observing the geyser from the veranda of the Old Faithful Inn in Yellowstone National Park. Remarkable in concept, the veranda is tucked under the gable and rests on massive stone piers with stripped tree trunks and branches for posts.

Figure 56 (above). Square porch posts were popular and easy to construct. They could be of solid wood, or boxed around with boards to increase their thickness, or hollow, put together with four mitered corner boards. The problem of injury from the sharp corners of the posts was minimized by a decorative, 45-degree chamfer or bevel. Classical capitals, bases, and pedestals could be suggested by applying combinations of panel boards and moldings.

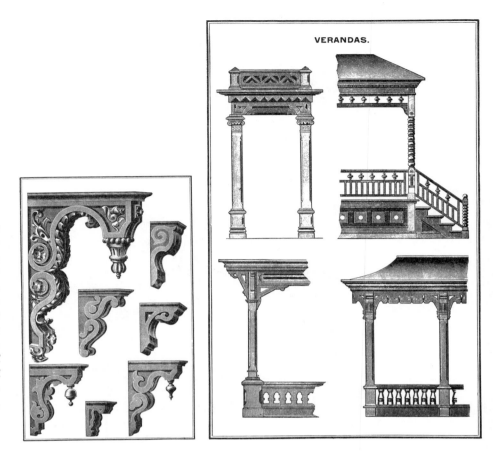

VERANDAS.

Figure 57 (above right). When it came to choosing brackets, there were many possibilities. Brackets could be cut from a 1½- to 2-inch-thick board or built up in a "sandwich" of three to five thinner boards. Additional ornament, usually floral, could then be incised, applied, or carved (see Fig. 41).

Figure 58 (above far right). Railings varied considerably, often using Renaissance and Gothic elements at the same time. Complex, pierced designs, similar to those of the Italian Villa style (see Fig. 43), were still popular, as were simple stick rails or vase-shaped turned rails that imitated the stone balustrade of a Renaissance palazzo.

apron. Rows of small brackets, often only six inches high, were sometimes placed under the porch cornice, as an additional decorative note (as in Fig. 43).

Porch rails, when used at all, were quite low by modern standards, often no more than the height of the paneled pedestal. Railing designs of Gothic or Renaissance influence varied from urn-shaped turned balustrades to complex pierced designs (Fig. 58).

In many cases, the entry porch was flat-roofed and formed an open, balustraded balcony. The porch ceiling was either left with structural members exposed or, according to one pattern book of the period, "ceiled with matched boards, smoothed and beaded."

Pattern books also showed how to carry an elaborate porch rail down the outside steps, finishing it off with a heavy newel post often eight to ten inches square. A set of carpenter's specifications published by A. J. Bicknell in 1872 calls for the porch steps to be built of "1¼ inch pine, ⅞" risers, 1¼ inch opened strings." The same source designates porch flooring to be made of "narrow 1¼ inch pine, laid in lead paint and neatly smoothed off and blind nailed, finished with a nosing and cone molding." Porch aprons were usually some sort of pierced board designs, although again, most have been replaced by ordinary lattice panels.

7

Romanesque,
1875–1895

The Romanesque-style house, strongly influenced by the work of the American architect Henry Hobson Richardson (1838–1886), resembled a medieval fortress with rough-faced masonry walls and deeply recessed doors and windows (Fig. 59). Heavy, semicircular arches with clearly defined voussoirs, squat columns with leafy or cushion-shaped capitals, and decorative corbeled brackets were all freely borrowed from eleventh- to thirteenth-century medieval and Syrian architecture. Round towers with conical roofs were characteristic, as were accenting bands of light-colored bricks or stone. Steeply pitched roofs were often hipped, with intersecting gables. The overall impression was of a building that had stood, or could stand, for many centuries (Fig. 60). Rows of narrow, single-paned windows with transoms, as well as the extensive use of stained glass and dark paneling, helped to create the rich but gloomy interiors characteristic of the period.

Because of its heavy masonry construction, the Romanesque house was expensive to build and never achieved the popularity of its contemporary, the Queen Anne style. It tended to be seen only in architect-designed, single-family homes or urban row houses. While there are many fine examples throughout the country, it was most prominent in the cities of the Northeast and Midwest.

The porch of the Romanesque house formed a dark and dramatic entryway, reflective of the fortresslike quality of the house itself. Rather than a wood frame appendage, the porch often matched the masonry body of the building itself. Although occasionally placed across the entire façade of the house, most Romanesque porches were set off to one side of the circular, corner tower (Fig. 61).

Figure 59. The prestigious New York firm of Rich and Lamb designed this solid, Romanesque-style house in Stamford, Connecticut, for a wealthy dealer in oriental art objects. Characterized by contrasting textures and materials, its gloomy appearance was typical of much post—Civil War architecture.

Figure 60. Massive walls with heavy, arched openings dominate C. D. Marvin's "Design for a City House," with its solid masonry balustrades and short, stubby columns.

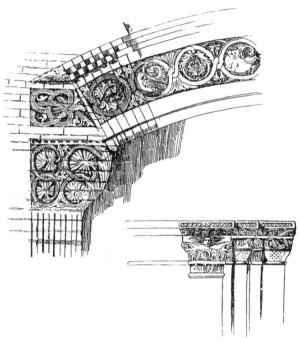

Figure 61 (left). Polygonal or cone-shaped corner towers gave Romanesque houses a picturesque, appropriately medieval air, enhanced by dark, mysterious porch openings often set within the main body of the house.

Sometimes an uncovered, second-story balcony was placed on top of a flat-roofed entry porch, protected by a stone or iron balcony rail. First- and second-story porches with arched openings were also set within the body of the house to form covered loggias.

Porch posts most frequently consisted of a row of squat, Romanesque-style columns set on top of a solid masonry parapet that rose directly from the ground. Other popular treatments included an arcade of rusticated stone arches or plain stone piers, sometimes even Classical columns. The Romanesque-style capitals were cushion-shaped or ornamented by leafy foliate designs (Fig. 62). Depending on their thickness, columns were placed singly or in pairs. Ornamental brackets were rarely used, as they were out of character with the general style.

Figure 62 (above). H. H. Richardson, the outstanding architect of the post–Civil War era, derived many of his decorative ideas from the richly carved, foliate ornament of twelfth-century French Romanesque churches.

8

Queen Anne,
1875–1900

The Philadelphia Centennial Exposition in 1876 brought the Queen Anne style to the attention of the American public, initiating a love affair that lasted almost twenty-five years. Referred to as the "Bric-a-Brac" style because of its free use of Classical detail on what would otherwise be a medieval-looking building, it made its first appearance among the avant-garde architects of the mid-nineteenth-century Arts and Crafts movement in England. During its quarter century of popularity, the Queen Anne style evolved from a half-timbered Elizabethan-looking prototype to a more Classical version incorporating Palladian decorative details.

Although Queen Anne houses came in many different formats, certain traits were common to them all. They featured steep, multigabled and turreted roof lines, an asymmetrical plan, and an emphasis upon textural variety and picturesque detail. Few surfaces were free from some form of embellishment. The lower story was usually covered in clapboard or brick, while bands of plain or scalloped shingles enlivened the upper floors. The gable was covered with a different shingle pattern, or made to look half timbered. Windows were usually combinations of clear plate glass surrounded by small, medieval-style panes of clear or colored glass. The heaviness of the forms was intensified by the rich, dark paint colors characteristic of the period (Fig. 63).

Except for the more authentic late-medieval versions of the Queen Anne, porches played a major role in the style. They were placed across the front of the house, or were L-shaped, or wrapped around three sides of the house. Second-story or sleeping porches were popular, as were

porte cocheres, extensions of the porch designed to provide a protective overhang for carriages. Polygonal, gazebolike structures were frequently used to accentuate the corners of the L-shaped porch.

In keeping with the medieval origins of the Queen Anne style, porch posts were turned, although now on power lathes instead of by hand. All kinds of turned posts were popular, utilizing many different arrangements of bulges and blocks (Fig. 64). Later versions of Queen Anne porch posts moved toward the Classical in design, and a modified version of the Tuscan column was popular (Fig. 65).

No one type of Queen Anne porch railing prevailed. While ornate turned posts became increasingly complex during this period, porch railings were sometimes simplified into a row of one-and-a-half-inch-square sticks (Fig. 66).

Brackets remained curvilinear, although not nearly as heavy or elaborate as those of the mid-Victorian era. Spindled porch lintels were popular, with some versions displaying lacy bands of spindles hung like fringe (Fig. 67). Toward the end of the century, as the Queen Anne style became

Figure 63. Henry R. Towne, a leading nineteenth-century hardware manufacturer, built this impressive mansion in 1879 within two blocks of the factory he owned in Stamford, Connecticut. Rockland, as it was called, captured the heavily textured, medieval quality of the early Queen Anne style, with its multiple gables and asymmetrically placed wings and chimney stacks.

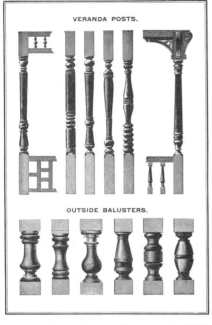

VERANDA POSTS.

OUTSIDE BALUSTERS.

Figure 64 (above). During the Middle Ages, as well as in the early New England colonies, hand-turned ornament played an important part. By the mid-nineteenth century, however, machinery could produce a dozen columns in the time it took to turn one post by hand. Catalogs and lumberyards now offered massproduced posts and spindles to be creatively arranged by a house builder in an almost infinite variety of patterns.

Figure 65 (above right). Later versions of Queen Anne–style porch posts moved away from the medieval "turned" variety toward the Classical. A modified, unfluted version of the Greek Doric column known as Tuscan was most often used.

Figure 66 (right). Railings were often formed by complex arrangements of horizontal and vertical sticks and panels, or were turned to match the porch posts. Porch stair rails terminated in heavy newel posts, often topped with ball-shaped finials.

VERANDAS.

VERANDAS.

Figure 67 (above). A spindled valance under the porch lintel echoed the complex turnings of the posts and rails and added to the heavily patterned look of the style. Similar rows of spindles were also used inside the house, defining the openings between the main rooms and the hall.

Figure 68 (left). The triangular pediment over the entry steps to the front porch could be embellished with a stylized sunburst or sunflower motif derived from the late-nineteenth-century English Arts and Crafts movement.

THE BACK PORCH

Although many fine historic houses, not the least of which is Mount Vernon, have handsome rear porches, the concept of a back porch has traditionally had other connotations. Until the universal adoption of indoor plumbing in the late nineteenth and early twentieth centuries, the back porch was not an especially pleasant environment for relaxation. It was primarily a work-

ing porch, or a "servant's porch" as the pattern books called it. It was an ideal place to perform household chores in warm weather, and provided a discreet means of exiting the house with the chamber pot. By the 1920s, however, indoor plumbing allowed the family full use of an insect- and odor-free porch and yard (Fig. 69).

Figure 69. H. Hudson Holly's Modern Dwellings in Town and Country *(1878) shows the maid carrying what might well be the contents of a chamber pot. It was important that such onerous chores be kept away from family and guests at the front of the house.*

more Classical, it abandoned brackets and spindle lintels for a frieze with applied dentils or garlands.

The porch entrance to the house was often defined by a separate gable. This triangular form could be turned into a Classical pediment, with or without ornament, or could be half-timbered, echoing the medieval treatment of the house gable (Fig. 68).

The porch ceiling was covered with narrow, beaded wood slats; these were often varnished, although a pale sky-blue paint color was also popular.

9

Shingle Style,
1880–1900

The Shingle Style is a mélange of late-nineteenth-century Queen Anne, Romanesque, Early Colonial, and Colonial Revival influences. Except for a number of architect-designed examples in the seaside resorts of the Northeast, it never became as popular as its contemporary, the Queen Anne (Fig. 70).

Shingle-style houses were distinguished by their continuous, uninterrupted skin of rough, unpainted wood shingles. The sweep of the shingled roof encompassed an array of intersecting gables, hips, gambrels, conical towers, and dormers, even reaching out over the side walls to form first- or second-story porches.

Large, rambling, and unpretentious, these houses relied on complex forms and natural textures to give them architectural interest, rather than applied or decorative ornament. Except for an occasional Palladian window, Classical column, or Romanesque arch, the Shingle style grew out of a renewed interest in the modest homes of the earliest colonial settlers.

The emphasis on natural materials created houses that would weather well in their seaside context: shingled walls, roofs, and porches turned a silver gray or a warm brown. When not shingled, the lower story of the house was covered by rough-textured rubble or cobblestone walls (Fig. 71). Windows were asymmetrically placed, either multipaned casement or double-hung, single panes of glass. Occasionally, a Palladian gable window, or a medieval leaded-glass stairway light added an ornamental note.

It is difficult to find a true Shingle-style house, as many were intermingled with the Queen Anne (Fig. 72) or Dutch Colonial Revival style (Fig. 73). Many architectural historians consider it the wooden version of

Figure 70. This house in Mount Desert, Maine, was designed by William Ralph Emerson in 1879 and may be the earliest Shingle-style residence in the country. It helped set a style for seaside cottages that became popular among architects building for an East Coast elite.

Figure 71. Rugged, heavy textures characterized the skin of the Shingle-style house. The lower story was often built of rough, unfinished stone, a practical, low-maintenance material for a seaside dwelling. The unpainted shingles that covered the remainder of the house also weathered well, turning a lustrous silver gray or dark brown after a number of years.

Figures 72, 73. It is difficult to find "pure" examples of the Shingle style, as most reflect the influence of contemporary Romanesque Revival, Queen Anne, or Dutch Colonial Revival architecture.

Figure 74. Second-story porches could be tucked into the main body of the house, serving as a healthy outdoor sleeping area adjacent to the bedrooms.

Figure 75. Shingle-style houses rarely used ornamental brackets. Instead, the effect of an arcade could be achieved by arching the shingle-covered piers.

the masonry Romanesque Revival. Additional confusion is created when the original shingles are covered by artificial siding, or when Stick- or Queen Anne—style houses are covered with shingles to give them an easily maintained, rustic Colonial look.

The porch of the Shingle-style house was viewed either as an extension of the rugged, natural-textured skin or as a contrasting note featuring white-painted Classical elements. In both cases, porches were dark and deep, perfect places to retire from the summer sun. Quite often, especially in the gambrel-roofed "Dutch" version, the porch was created by extending the main roof beyond the walls of the house, or by tucking the porch underneath the second story of the house (Fig. 74). This helped create a desirable connection between exterior and interior space. These verandas accented the horizontal lines of the house, and stretched along one entire side or curved around two sides. A conical- or polygonal-roofed gazebo often marked the corner of an L-shaped porch. In any case, porches were placed so as to take advantage of the best breezes and views, rather than to follow any predetermined order.

Porch posts were heavy and dramatic, usually avoiding the fussy turnings of the Queen Anne style. They were often covered with shingles or made of stone to match the main body of the house (see Fig. 71). Sometimes they formed a row of wide, semicircular arches reflective of late-nineteenth-century Romanesque influences (Fig. 75). Also popular were plain wood posts, or simple, Tuscan-style columns, occasionally resting on paneled wood bases.

The porch balustrade reflected the overall architectural character of the posts. At times, it was a solid, shingled balustrade, at other times, an arrangement of simple one-and-a-half-inch sticks, or turned balusters. One popular treatment featured a stone balustrade that was an extension of the foundation itself. When Queen Anne elements were applied to a Shingle-style structure, one will find turned posts and rails, sometimes even spindle valances under the porch lintel.

Porches stood fairly close to the ground, with lattice panels or extensions of the rough stone foundation protecting the underside. Porch ceilings were covered with narrow, beaded slats, varnished rather than painted for easier maintenance in a shorefront setting.

10

Bungalow or Craftsman Style, 1890–1920

The Bungalow- or Craftsman-style house developed as an alternative to the fussy Eclectic Revivals of the early twentieth century, and dominated the small-house market for many years. Its low-pitched gable with overhanging eaves and exposed rafter ends expressed the Arts and Crafts movement's preference for rugged forms and natural materials (Fig. 76).

Originally derived from the "bangla" houses of English-ruled India (Fig. 77), the one-and-a-half-story Bungalow reflected a wide variety of other stylistic influences, including Tudor, Colonial, Oriental, Adirondack Log Cabin (Fig. 78), and Spanish Mission (Fig. 79). A flood of Bungalow

Figure 76. The cozy, one-and-a-half-story bungalow had nationwide appeal. As long as it was small in scale, and the materials "natural looking," i.e., rough shingles, logs, or masonry, it could be adapted to many different stylistic variations.

·A·SMALL·BUNGALOW·

Figure 77. *The East Indian "bangla," the one-story native house brought back to England by retiring civil servants, eventually reached its greatest popularity in the United States. This drawing, taken from* Appleton's Home Book *(1881), illustrates the native origins of the bungalow.*

Figure 78. *Covered in rough chestnut logs and boards, this rustic bungalow was especially popular in mountain resort areas such as the Adirondacks. The screened porch on the left provided an outdoor dining area with an often-glorious view.*

Figure 79. *Californians preferred Spanish Mission—style bungalows as closest to their heritage and hearts. Stuccoed walls and curvilinear, Baroque gables gave architectural character to this otherwise modest two-bedroom house, the plans for which could be purchased for twelve dollars and mailed "the same day the order is received."*

Figure 80. This "simple and home-like" bungalow could be erected in 1913 for $2,600. The open, pergola-type porch and the tall French windows gave more light to the front rooms than was usual in bungalows, which tended to have dark interiors (see Figs. 81 and 82).

pattern books emanated from California, offering full sets of plans sometimes for less than ten dollars. More elaborate, architect-designed versions known as Craftsman-style houses also appeared throughout the country, although the best examples, as is true of the Bungalow, can be found in southern California.

Wood shingles were the most popular exterior covering, however many houses used brick or stucco. Shingles were left to weather in their natural state or were stained dark. Window styles varied and included both casement or sash, with either a single pane of glass or many smaller panes. In keeping with the idea of integrating the house with its environment, foundations and chimneys were made of rugged-looking cobblestone or fieldstone.

Bungalow- and Craftsman-style houses were among the last twentieth-century building types to regard the front porch as essential. Deep, shaded porches were created by extending the front gable out to create a wide porch. Unfortunately, these wide porches were designed for sunny climates, and had a tendency to darken the interior of the house. Since this was not always desirable, one suggested solution was to construct the porch with an open, trellislike roof, which could be covered by vines or an awning (Fig. 80).

Porch posts varied considerably, but were generally shorter and heavier than those of Victorian or Colonial Revival origin. Rough-cut stone piers were popular, as were tapered wood posts, or sturdy columns in the Doric/ Tuscan style (Figs. 81, 82). Other variations included stuccoed or shingled piers, or shingle-covered arches. Posts frequently rested on massive stone piers that extended to the ground or on solid, shingle-covered or stone balustrades. Wooden rails, when used, were rather plain, "Craftsman"-style slats, five to seven inches wide (Fig. 83), occasionally with cutout geometric designs or a row of one- to one-and-a-half-inch sticks.

Figures 81, 82. Heavy, stuccoed columns added a fashionable Classical touch to a style that was otherwise devoid of Classical influence. The pattern book plans for the house shown in Fig. 81 (at left) may well have been the source for this bungalow (below) in Greenwich, Connecticut.

Figure 83. In keeping with the Bungalow style's preference for rugged siding materials, porch posts, brackets, and rails also emphasized a hand-hewn look. Flat board rails were often used in combination with heavy posts and angle braces.

11

Eclectic Revivals, 1890–1940

While the public's fondness for Colonial architecture began with the Centennial Exposition in Philadelphia in 1876, Colonial Revival and other Eclectic styles did not take full hold until the end of the century. Unlike the relatively free architectural revivals of the Victorian era, early-twentieth-century revivals stressed greater historical accuracy (Fig. 84). Beginning with mansions and manor houses, Eclectic architecture filtered down through the ranks of American society, ending up in low-priced pattern books as stylistic shadows of their former selves. Every American town and suburb soon had hundreds of modest cottages that mimicked the façades of Old and New World landmarks. This desire for historical roots dominated American home building until the Depression of the 1930s put a halt to construction nationwide until after World War II.

Although porches were still commonplace, they were rarely as important as in the previous era. When a front porch conflicted with the historical authenticity of the Revival style, it might be relegated to other, less visible parts of the house. Eclectic-period houses instead might include side, rear, or sleeping porches (Fig. 85).

The Colonial Revival Style, 1880–1940

The Colonial Revival can be broken down to at least a half-dozen substyles, some of which are rather fanciful interpretations of the original Georgian or Federal house (Fig. 86). Others were eclectic mixtures: Colonial Revival and Queen Anne (Fig. 87), box-shaped "Foursquare" houses with hipped roofs, or gambrel-roofed "Dutch" Colonials (Fig. 88). In fact, Colonial Revivals of one sort or another are still being built today.

Figure 84. Beaux Arts—trained or —influenced American architects were encouraged to design houses for wealthy clients in Eclectic styles such as Mediterranean, Renaissance, Tudor, Chateauesque, or, as in this example from Evanston, Illinois, a Neo-Classical form of Colonial Revival.

Figure 85. This 1927 attempt to imitate a modest late-eighteenth-century or early-nineteenth-century Colonial dwelling made the use of a front porch historically inaccurate. Since large suburban lots minimized interchange with passersby anyway, a porch could just as easily be eliminated or tucked to the side or rear of the house.

Figure 86. This early 1900s Colonial Revival house in Glen Ridge, New Jersey, features applied garlands, a form of ornament derived from late-eighteenth-century Adamesque architecture. Garlands were applied to the frieze of this hipped-roof box with its rooftop balustrade. The triple-columned entry porch with a balcony above was designed to impress a visitor, rather than to provide an informal, outdoor room.

Figure 87. Although Queen Anne–style houses were still built as late as 1910, they increasingly incorporated Colonial Revival features. This 1909 plan book design, with its Classical pediment, still retains the picturesque tipped roof and curvilinear porch brackets of the now-unfashionable Queen Anne.

Figure 88. Although referred to as the Dutch Colonial Revival style, houses such as this one in Elizabeth, New Jersey, bear only passing resemblance to the actual dwellings of Dutch or German colonial settlers. The gambrel roof was also popular in the English colonies in the late eighteenth century, while the use of Palladian and Adamesque ornament and a Classical columned porch further muddied the stylistic waters.

Although the more historically accurate reproductions of eighteenth-century houses had no porch at all, most Colonial Revivals displayed porches with Classical columns in a wide variety of sizes and configurations. They could be oval-shaped, rectangular, or semicircular and were often impressively large (Fig. 89). Colossal, two-story porticoes reappeared from time to time (see Fig. 84), sometimes with segmentally arched or full triangular pediments. Unfluted Doric (Tuscan), Ionic, and Corinthian columns were commonplace, set in pairs or triples (see Fig. 86) and resting on solid, shingle-covered balustrades. Other railings were made of turned balusters or simple one-and-a-half-inch-wide sticks, sometimes set in intricate patterns.

Pedimented entryways were popular, especially in the Federal version of the Colonial Revival style. Their purpose was to define the entrance to the front porch, and they were embellished by traditional Classical elements such as Doric columns or a dentiled frieze (Fig. 90).

Colonial Revival houses frequently had a flat-roofed porch with a balustraded second-story balcony on top of it. Balcony rails were quite elaborate, with corner pedestals or newel posts (Fig. 95). The increasing use of screened or glassed-in sleeping porches reflected the prevailing belief in the healthfulness of fresh air, even in winter (see Fig. 74).

Figure 89 (above left). Design elements from early-nineteenth-century Federal architecture were used in the oval entry portico of this suburban house. The curved entablature, the "Chippendale" balustrade, and the Temple of the Winds columns are all part of a mishmash of Eclectic elements applied to an otherwise plain brick structure.

Figure 90 (above right). By introducing a few feet of Classical molding over a pair of attenuated Tuscan columns, this simple, gabled entry porch acquired architectural importance and a link with similar structures of the Colonial era.

ENCLOSURES, SCREENS, AND AWNINGS

Next to tearing down the entire porch, inappropriate or unattractive porch enclosures are the most common visual "injury" to a historic house. A stroll down a typical suburban street discloses a wide variety of porch enclosures, ranging from the popular "Florida," or glass-louvered, porch to almost total encapsulation in vinyl or wood.

Is there any way to expand the usefulness of the front porch without sacrificing its appearance?

Victorian porches were often enclosed during the winter by means of *temporary*, attached panels of muntined glass (see Fig. 59), placed *behind* the porch columns and rails. Although a modern treatment might require the use of large sheets of plate glass, muntined panels tend to harmonize well with the multipaned windows of an older house. Small panes of glass are also cheaper to buy, install, and repair. In some cases, permanent enclosures do work well, but great care has to be taken to ensure that the overall architectural character of the house is not compromised (Fig. 91).

In general, we recommend removable porch enclosures, which can be changed with the seasons. This is the most historically accurate way to enclose a front porch, and the least disruptive to the appearance of the house. If you need additional all-year-round living space, build an addition where it can't be seen from the street. Turning the front or side porch into an enclosed room never works very well, from either an aesthetic or a practical point of view.

Screening the front porch also raises design issues. For comfort, large, removable porch screens are certainly a welcome solution to the warm-weather insect problem. Russell Lynes, in his book *The Domesticated American*, refers to the invention of window screening in the 1880s as

the "most humane contribution the 19th century made to the preservation of sanity and good temper." Although screened porches tend to darken the interior rooms, this is probably quite desirable in warmer weather, as long as you can take the screens off during the colder months of the year.

Before the invention of large metal screens, wooden "venetian" blinds, shutters, or draped fabric panels were placed between the columns of the porch (Fig. 92). Blinds and shutters not only kept the heat of the day away from the house, but helped discourage the many insects that plagued the American home, especially in the South.

The use of canvas for roof coverings appears to date back to the late eighteenth century when striped awning fabric was applied to the roofs of entry porches. In the early 1800s, sheet-metal porch roofs were painted in wide stripes to represent awning fabric in a more permanent form (see Fig. 16).

Awnings, shades, and latticework were popular and easy ways to shield the house or porch from excessive sunlight, but are rarely seen in the age of electric fans and air-conditioning (Figs. 93, 94). Awnings, whether on porch or windows, provide a soft, shaded light without blocking the view. Early-twentieth-century houses especially were designed to have awnings, and their removal eliminates a vital finishing touch.

Figure 91 (opposite). The enclosed porch at Lyndhurst, a Gothic Revival mansion in Tarrytown, New York, was an informal parlor where Helen Gould, daughter of railroad magnate Jay Gould, could converse with friends in 1909.

Figure 92 (top). Lavish draperies and fringed, striped canvas awnings frame the two-story semicircular veranda in this elegant 1907 photograph of an American Neo-Renaissance villa.

Figure 93 (above). This 1930s version of a Colonial farmhouse was enlivened by historically inaccurate but pleasingly striped canvas awnings.

Figure 94 (right). In his widely read pattern book Villas and Cottages, *published in 1863, Calvert Vaux demonstrated how lattice and vines could be used to provide privacy ". . . with but little sacrifice of light." He also encouraged his readers to use their ingenuity with lattice and "readily arrange new varieties of pattern to embody the same general idea."*

DESIGN FOR PARTIALLY INCLOSED VERANDA.

Figure 95. An imposing Colonial Revival porch or balcony required a heavy molded hand rail with turned or stick rails. Every six or eight feet the rail was interrupted by posts, pedestals, or columns. Ball or urn finials provided an appropriate finishing touch to the posts.

~North ~Elevation~
Residence ~ for
~ Mr & Mrs Charles Porter Wilson ~
~ Mill Neck, L.I.

Hart & Shape
Architects
247 Park Ave N.Y.C.

J. MacGilchrist

Figure 96. By living in a Tudor house, an ambitious homeowner could acquire "instant ancestry," and a connection to the English gentry. Improvements in masonry building techniques now allowed a simple stick-frame house to take on the look of masonry half-timber construction.

Some of these buildings were so closely patterned after eighteenth-century originals that seventy or eighty years later it is difficult to tell which is the original and which is the copy. In addition, many nineteenth-century Victorian houses were "Colonial Revival-ed" by having their gingerbread removed and replaced by recycled or replicated Colonial details (see Chapter 13). As in the Queen Anne style, porch ceilings were covered with narrow, beaded wood slats, varnished or painted a sky blue.

Tudor Revival, 1890–1940

The Tudor Revival was one of the most popular early-twentieth-century Eclectic house styles. While theoretically based on early-sixteenth-century English architecture, the style is actually taken from a wide variety of late medieval and early Renaissance sources. Although a number of high-style, half-timbered versions appeared before World War I, it did not achieve full acceptance until the 1920s and 1930s, when improvements in masonry veneer encouraged its widespread use. Tudor Revivals were so prevalent in the wealthier suburbs that the style was derisively referred to as "Stockbroker Tudor" (Fig. 96).

In general, Tudor Revival was characterized by steep, front-facing gables with false half-timbering, and brick, stone, or stucco walls. Tall, narrow casement windows with small, diamond-shaped or rectangular panes of leaded glass were often placed in groups of three or more. Large, elaborate chimneys were also favorite details, often with separate chimney pots, one for each fireplace. Entries were important, and a flattened Tudor arch was frequently used over the door or on the arched openings of the entry porch.

Since twentieth-century Revival architecture emphasized greater historical accuracy, the front porch was either eliminated or reduced to the status of a small entry porch. Porches were incorporated, however, into rear or side elevations and became screened or glassed-in extensions of the main parlor. As the porch now rested only one or two steps off the ground and was partially enclosed, it required no railing. Porch posts were usually heavy, rough-cut timbers with angled braces echoing the medieval half-timbering of the gable (Fig. 97).

Spanish Colonial Revival, 1915–1940

Spanish Colonial Revival was another of the Eclectic house styles that dominated early-twentieth-century suburbs. It originated in the turn-of-the-century Spanish Mission style, reached its peak during the 1920s and 1930s, and passed rapidly out of favor by World War II. Although houses

Figure 97. Since actual dwellings in fifteenth- and sixteenth-century England rarely had anything other than small entry porches, twentieth-century Tudor Revivals kept the porch as inconspicuous as possible. Instead of Classical columns and rails, they featured rough wood posts with angled timber braces.

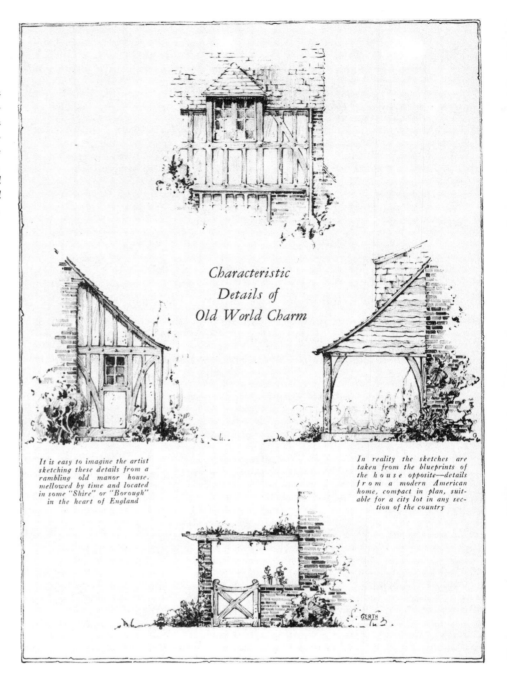

Characteristic Details of Old World Charm

It is easy to imagine the artist sketching these details from a rambling old manor house, mellowed by time and located in some "Shire" or "Borough" in the heart of England

In reality the sketches are taken from the blueprints of the house opposite—details from a modern American home, compact in plan, suitable for a city lot in any section of the country

of this type were built throughout the country, the best examples are found in the warm climates of the southwestern states and in Florida. Spanish Colonial Revival houses are generally identified by their stucco or plaster walls and low-pitched, red tile roofs (Fig. 98); they also featured massive, heavily carved entry doors set into elaborate door frames. Small-paned casement windows, sometimes arched, were popular, and many houses had at least one dramatically placed, focal-point window (Fig. 99). Other decorative elements included iron window grilles, balconies, and lanterns.

Eclectic in detail, decorative motifs were borrowed from the entire range of Mediterranean architecture: Moorish, medieval, and Renais-

Figure 98 (above). This architect-designed residence in Pasadena, California, makes use of traditional Spanish Colonial architecture, including a low tile roof and a second-story, balcony-type porch with a cast-iron rail.

Figure 99 (left). The Spanish Colonial Revival house could also be adapted for suburban living. Hollow-tile walls with a stucco finish provided a great deal of charm at a reasonable cost. In this example entitled "Spanish for the Two-Story House," a pair of dramatic arched windows light the two-story living room with its beamed ceiling and wrought-iron balcony.

Figure 100. An arcaded, loggia-type porch could be properly set within the body of the house. Furnished with wicker, a paddle fan, and hanging plants, this example successfully evokes the ambience of a Mediterranean villa.

UPPER-STORY PORCHES

"It seems to me that no happier solution of the problem is to be found for the city prisoner than that of the second-story veranda, or we might call it the 'upstairs veranda,' and so not limit its level. Naturally the dwellers in warmer climates than ours were the first to discover the delights of such open-air rooms as roof gardens and loggias, and the most familiar classic model for the present day veranda is the Italian loggia and that, more often than not, is found upon the upper levels of the house.

"For the average modern house this retreat, if it is to serve as the gathering place of the family and their resort for the drinking of afternoon tea, is more practicable if built on the level of the second floor. And here, if the veranda be large enough, one may almost live a complete cycle of life, reading or sewing, sleeping, eating and talking, at peace with one's friends, far removed from the bustle and dust of the highway and the intrusive gaze of the curious or unduly interested passerby. And for the practical minded it is an excellent place in winter, when the ground is bad, for the thrifty housewife to have her rugs beaten and shaken." (From *Indoors and Out*, July 1907)

sance. While architect-designed houses had a greater degree of historical accuracy, the popularly priced versions derived from builders' pattern books mixed influences with considerable abandon. Rather than attach a conventional porch to the front of the house, Spanish Colonial Revival buildings often featured arched loggia-type porches, set within the walls themselves (Fig. 100). These loggias were composed of round or pointed arches resting on masonry columns or stucco-covered piers. Second-story balcony porches, covered by an extension of the main roof, were also popular, and featured wooden or cast- or wrought-iron rails.

One- or two-story covered porches were often found on the back of the house, serving as a shaded exterior passage between rooms. Heavy wooden posts with simple curved or angle brackets also gave an appropriately informal look to these atrium-type verandas.

12

Prairie Style,
1900–1920

A distinctively American form of residential architecture, the Prairie style was developed at the turn of the century by a group of Chicago architects, including Frank Lloyd Wright. Rejecting academic influences, Wright and his colleagues created a simple style, respectful of vernacular building traditions and local materials yet artistic and innovative (Fig. 102). Their work came to be called the Prairie School and was associated with what Wright referred to as "organic architecture, . . . unfolding or growing from the inside out, establishing integral relationships between plan and external expression, architecture and decoration."

Pattern-book adaptations of the Prairie style were popular throughout the country, especially in the Midwest. Houses were typically two stories high, with low hipped roofs and wide overhanging eaves. Details such as cornices, string courses, and lined-up rows of windows emphasized the basic horizontal orientation of the building. Since the style had its origin in the American version of the English Arts and Crafts movement, Prairie-style houses were designed to look as if they were made from the materials at hand: stucco, brick, or stained wood (Fig. 103). Windows were casement or double-hung, with leaded or small panes of glass designed to give the appropriate medieval hand-crafted look.

Applied ornament was derived from natural or geometric forms; yet, in contrast with Arts and Crafts movement philosophy, the architects who used these natural materials also embraced engineering technology, building with machine-made terra-cotta and concrete blocks and using steel beams to cantilever roofs and balconies.

A popular hybrid version of the Prairie style was the American Foursquare, a hipped-roof, boxlike building that combined Colonial Revival

Figure 102. In Prairie-style dwellings such as the Gayle House in Oak Park, Illinois, porches and balconies were an integral part of the house, rather than ornamental "afterthoughts." The broad, overhanging eaves sheltered interior rooms from the hot summer sun while still retaining sunlight and views.

Figure 104. *In this design from Radford's Portfolio of Plans, published in 1909, the stucco used for the finish and ornament of the porch posts and balustrades is the same as used for the main body of the house, further emphasizing their relationship.*

details with the overall horizontal emphasis and simplicity of the Prairie style.

Porches and balconies were frequently used to enhance the Prairie style's avowed connection with its environment. These porches tended to be one story high, and occasionally were covered by the projecting overhang of the main roof. Porch piers or posts were generally of wood or masonry, either square or tapered at the top. A low masonry parapet wall or a modest stick rail provided an unpretentious balustrade (Fig 104).

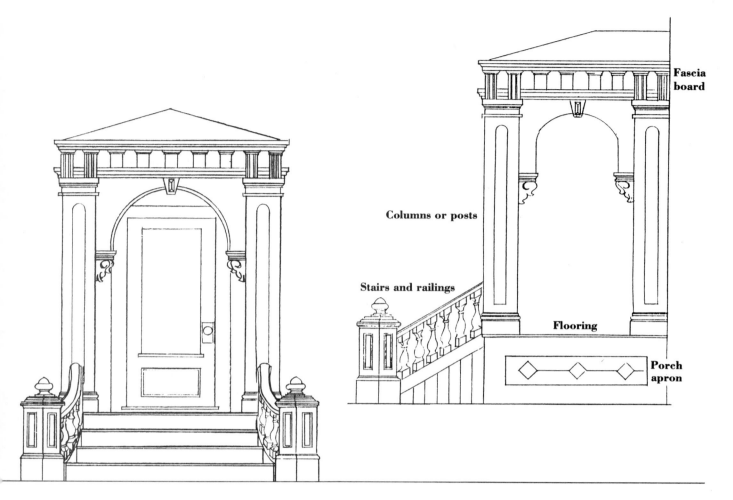

Fascia
board

Columns or posts

Stairs and railings

Flooring

Porch
apron

PART TWO

13

Researching Your Porch

If all you want to do is patch and paint, fixing up a porch is fairly simple. If you're careful about good craftsmanship and use top-quality materials, you should be able to restore your porch to its original condition without too much trouble.

But what if the porch needs more than patch and paint? What if it was removed and no one remembers what it looked like? Or if it's missing posts or rails or brackets? In order to know what to put back, you're going to have to figure out what was originally there. This involves finding out the date the house was built, when and if it was remodeled, what style it is, and what physical evidence exists for you to follow.

To complicate matters, houses are not just works of art but functional entities. Over the years, rooms have been added or subtracted, entrances moved, rooflines raised, and windows replaced. If you own a hundred-year-old house, the chances are that a good fifty percent or more of the exterior is not original to the house. That is not to say it doesn't replicate what was there, but houses were always being "modernized" with whatever was fashionable at the time.

Porches, vulnerable as they are to weather damage, are among the most frequently altered features of an older house. You have even more problems with a building that dates back to Colonial times. A porch of one sort or another may have been added or subtracted several times over the past two hundred or more years (Fig. 105).

The first piece of information you need to know is when the house was actually built; this will help determine its basic style. If it's pre-1900, some information may be available at your local historical society or library. Check with your State Historical Commission to see if it is listed

Figure 105. Houses are as subject to the whims of fashion as clothing. During the early Victorian era, "bare and bald" Colonial houses were updated by the addition of ornate gingerbread porches and gables. By the beginning of the twentieth century, however, the process reversed itself, and the desire for Colonial-era simplicity and restrained ornament caused many Victorian houses to be stripped of trim.

on a Historic Resources Inventory. If you get nowhere with these sources, you'll have to do some digging of your own.

Your next stop is the town clerk's office. Check your assessment card, but don't expect it to be too accurate, if it has any information at all. Most municipalities didn't require building plans to be filed until the 1950s. We had one experience where houses were simply and unhelpfully described as "old" or "very old" on city records. Another time, we found that many of the cards listed dates ending in the number two—1892 or 1842; we soon realized that the cards were originally made out in 1942, and the field assessor was only guessing that the house was "around" fifty or one hundred years old.

Next try the land sale records. By going from grantor to grantee, you should be able to get back to the date of construction of your house, or at least an approximation. You'll find the sale records say "land and dwelling" until you get to one that just says "land." That's where your house probably comes in. Or at least we *hope* it's your house. This process should be fairly rapid and easy, even for a novice, unless you get into complicated land transactions or confusing plot lines. . . . Then, you're going to need expert help, and may never come up with a definitive answer.

To make matters worse, many towns don't even *have* land records. They were lost through fire, water damage, or just plain neglect. If that's the case, we often turn to old maps. Most areas have maps dating back to colonial times, some with little drawings of the houses themselves. They don't help much in rural areas but often give detailed information on urban properties, including height, roof type, covering material, *and* size and placement of porches. The Sanborn fire insurance maps are especially helpful. Beginning in 1867 and updated until 1961, these maps provided detailed information on over 12,000 cities and towns in North America. If your local library or town clerk's office doesn't have them, check the Library of Congress to see what is available.

The Library of Congress also has a listing of the panoramic bird's-eye-view maps that were popular from 1850 to the early 1900s. These hand-drawn aerial views clearly portray buildings, streets, and landscape, and are remarkable for their thoroughness and accuracy (Fig. 106).

You can get an approximate date of construction for your house by noting when it first appeared on a map. If it's not on the 1867 map but *is* on the 1879 map, the house was probably built during that twelve-year interval . . . unless, of course, it was an older house moved to the site from another location. The "waste not, want not" Yankee did a lot more moving of houses in those days than we do today.

One way to determine when additions or remodeling took place is to check the town tax records. A jump in assessment usually suggests something significant happened to the house in that particular year.

After coming up with an approximate date of construction, you are

Figure 106. In the nineteenth century, most American towns and cities commissioned "aerial" views such as this detail of one of Stamford, Connecticut, published in 1883. Designed to look as if drawn from a balloon, these panoramas provide remarkably detailed and accurate townscapes, and can usually be relied upon for information such as roof shape, number of bays, size and placement of porches, and natural features including trees and ponds.

now ready to tackle the question of style. An accurate date helps, but you can also base your determination on the physical appearance of the house. Check Part I, the style section of this book, or consult some of the other, more detailed guides listed in the bibliography. But remember, houses are not scientifically categorized flora and fauna. With few exceptions, they refuse to fit into neat pigeonholes. Despite the fact that most older houses were derived from pattern-book illustrations, they were rarely totally faithful to the original. Carpenters and owners often added eccentric or personal details; there were also regional variations, many related to local building materials or climate. Styles didn't begin and end suddenly; they started earlier in the fashionable cities and lingered longer in rural, backwater areas. Styles were often mixed within the same house, and it is not uncommon to see buildings of the mid-1800s, for example, that exhibit Gothic, Italianate, and Greek Revival characteristics within the same structure. Houses were often remodeled every few decades, and what you have now may bear very little resemblance to what was originally there.

Once you have established a date and an approximate stylistic category, you can begin to look for some information about the porch itself. Here are some suggestions as to how to proceed.

1. Search for physical evidence on the house itself. Missing pieces often leave behind "ghost marks," lines that indicate where something

was removed. You can often tell the shape of a missing porch or see where trim was removed by looking for marks on the remaining structure. If the house has been re-sided, you might have to remove some of the later covering to check what's underneath.

It's a pleasant surprise when you find that missing pieces were saved by some thrifty homeowner for use at a later date. We have discovered original posts and brackets stored in attics and basements. Once we found an entire ornamental porch rail behind the lattice, while a grim sheet of unpainted plywood was nailed up to take its place. One house we worked on had had its graceful Ionic columns stolen. Fortunately, the thieves left one column standing—not out of any conscience, they just didn't want the porch roof to fall down on them. From the sole remaining column we were able to replicate the others, but at considerable trouble and expense.

2. If physical evidence on the house itself doesn't tell you what you want to know, look around the neighborhood and explore nearby towns. Just as today, builders often used one set of plans over and over again . . . or bought their decorative details from the same lumberyard or catalog. By carefully observing houses that are similar to yours, you may come up with the answers you are looking for. For example, one house may still have the original porch posts but has lost its brackets; another may have the brackets but have pressure-treated lumber sticks in place of the original posts. Still a third house has what appears to be an original railing.

3. One of the best ways to learn about the historical appearance of your house and porch is to look for period photographs (Figs. 107, 108). Historical societies and libraries usually have extensive archives, although they may not be in the most accessible order. The photograph needn't even be of your house, just something similar. Remember though that the picture might show later modifications and not be the house at the time of its construction. One local restorer botched a good job when he painted his Greek Revival "temple" in the dark colors he had seen in an 1880s photograph. The photo was taken some forty years after the building was built, and did not reflect the pale, marblelike colors of the original.

4. Talk to your neighbors. Oral histories and reminiscences are notoriously unreliable, but they do give you important leads to check out. We learned, for example, that our own 1832 farmhouse once had a full front Victorian porch—it now has a neo-Colonial rear porch. Another neighbor came up with an old photograph he had of our house after a fire in the attic. It clearly showed an elaborate Victorian gable ornament probably removed when the house was "Colonialized" back in the 1930s.

5. After you have a fairly good—if general—idea of the basic style of your house, you're ready to head for the local bookstore or library. Thanks to reprint houses such as Dover Publications and the American Life Foundation, you can find many fine replicas of eighteenth-, nineteenth-, and twentieth-century pattern books (see the Bibliography). Not

Figures 107, 108. According to a photograph taken in 1892, this rather uninteresting house once had a great deal of architectural character. Its wide, L-shaped veranda with cutwork rails was removed when the road was widened in the 1970s, while a "quick and easy" re-siding did away with any remaining period detail.

only do they illustrate entire houses, but they clearly show details of porch posts, rails, and brackets. A good carpenter should be able to work from these drawings.

If you can't find appropriate reprints, you'll have to look for copies of original pattern books. A college library will be able to help you, and interlibrary loans can be arranged. It's even easier with a twentieth-century house, as there are lots of home-building magazines you can turn to. Many libraries have complete runs dating back to the turn of the century, and a small duplicating fee will bring you copies of the articles you need.

6. One of the most important and difficult decisions you will have to make is whether or not to restore your house to the way it looked at the time it was built. There is no one answer to this question, and what you do depends on a number of factors. After all, a house that has been around for a hundred years or more is entitled to some changes. If you are doing a museum-type restoration, you might want to go back to an authentic, original appearance. Otherwise, what is on the house now may be a lot more attractive and interesting than what used to be there, and you're better off leaving it alone (Figs. 109, 110).

One final bit of advice: Working with old buildings brings to mind Mies van der Rohe's dictum that "God is in the details." Restoring an old building is a labor of love. You can't do it quickly, easily, or cheaply. If you try to save money by using modern-sized lumber or skimpy, ready-made trim, the finished product is never going to look right. A costly restoration can be marred by a penny-wise decision to go with something that's cheaper and "almost as good." If nothing else, the people who built these old houses usually gave good measure for their money. That's why they lasted so long, sometimes despite almost total neglect. If you are not ready to do what needs to be done, or spend what needs to be spent, please wait, or sell the house to someone who will do it justice.

Figures 109, 110. Fig. 109 (left) is a vernacular Greek Revival house, probably built around 1840, with an added Victorian porch. A Civil War—era photo of a similar house in a nearby town (right) shows us how the house may have originally looked. This leaves the homeowner with an interesting dilemma! Does he want to show the architectural changes that have taken place over a century and a half, or does he want an accurate replication of the original appearance?

14

Porch Maintenance and Repair

Older porches are rarely problem-free. They are subjected to all extremes of weather as well as insect attack. Some of this deterioration will be obvious, like the blistering or peeling paint that points to water damage. But some is very insidious, and the entire porch requires careful inspection and thoughtful evaluation. You should methodically check wood members in the following areas for water and insect damage:

1. the underside or substructure of the porch
2. flooring, especially at the ends
3. stairs and railings, especially at ground level
4. porch aprons, especially where they are in contact with the ground
5. columns and posts, especially at the base
6. under the roof or porch ceiling, where moisture stains may be found
7. where the porch connects to the house
8. the fascia board behind the gutters for dampness
9. gutters and downspouts

The only unpleasant part of the inspection—a venture into the crawl space beneath the porch—is also the most important. Don't avoid it! It is the only way to assess fully a porch's condition. Look at the bright side: one of the advantages of this damp journey may be that you discover signs of the original footprint of your porch or profiles of trim work. (See Chapter 13.)

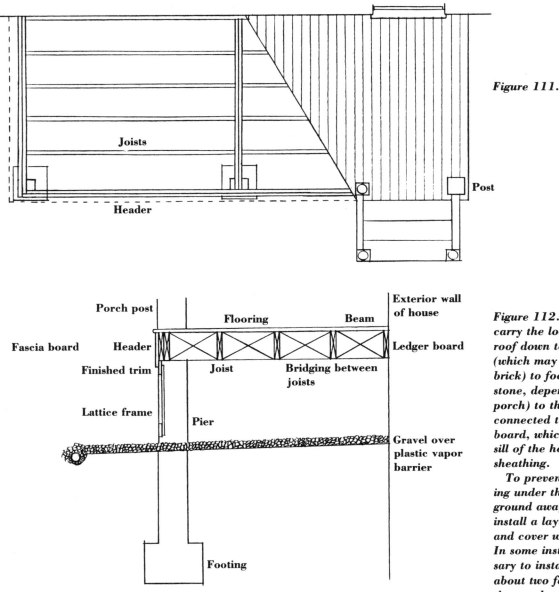

Figure 111.

Joists

Header

Post

Porch post

Flooring

Beam

Exterior wall
of house

Fascia board   Header

Ledger board

Finished trim

Joist

Bridging between
joists

Lattice frame

Pier

Gravel over
plastic vapor
barrier

Footing

The Substructure

Although rarely seen and little appreciated, the substructure, or the area beneath the flooring, is as elemental to the life of the porch as the delicate tracery of the lattice (Fig. 111). Although the substructure is comparatively sturdy, it is susceptible to several blights that, if not repaired or corrected, may considerably shorten the life span of the porch.

The substructure supports the weight of the porch, distributing the load evenly to the ground. The usual structural components are simple: footings, piers or supports, floor joists, the sill or ledger board connecting the porch to the house, and the header joists spanning from pier to pier. Maintenance of these areas is of primary importance, given their inherent susceptibility to damage from water, insects, and differential settlement of the ground around the foundation (Fig. 112).

Figure 112. Porch posts or columns carry the load of the floor and the roof down to the ground via piers (which may be wood, stone, or brick) to footings (concrete or stone, depending on the age of the porch) to the ground. The porch is connected to the house at the ledger board, which may be bolted to the sill of the house or the exterior sheathing.

To prevent water from accumulating under the porch, slope the ground away from the house wall, install a layer of plastic sheeting, and cover with two inches of gravel. In some instances, it may be necessary to install perforated pvc pipe about two feet from the perimeter of the porch to lead excess water away from the porch.

Footing depth is determined by state building code. The size of the footing is determined by the amount of the weight the footing must support. Calculations for the size of the footing and all of the structures should take into consideration the weight of the structure, the weight of the people using the porch and the furniture, etc., placed on the porch, as well as the weight of snow and ice, wind load, and other weather conditions.

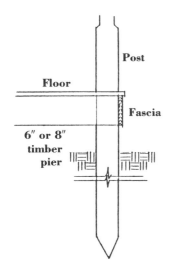

Figure 113. A wooden pier would have been buried directly in the ground.

Figure 114. A standard masonry pier with mortar joints.

Figure 115. Dry stone masonry: no mortar is used to bind the stones; instead, the friction of the stones' surface and the interlocking of the pieces hold the stones in place.

Historically, three types of materials were used to support the weight of the porch: wood posts, stone piers, or brick piers. Wood posts were simply driven into the ground and the porch structure was built above them (Fig. 113). Because of wood's vulnerability, few examples of this type of support have survived. Masonry (stone or brick) piers were built in one of two ways. The builder would either excavate the ground at the area of support until a firm bedrock foundation was found on which to build the pier or, if none was found, create a footing of rubblestone (rock piled up as a base). A stone pier would likely have been constructed with mortar joints (Fig. 114), although dry stone masonry piers (no mortar joints) are possible (Fig. 115). Historic brick piers were constructed with soft sandy mortar, much softer than the commercial mortar mixes available today. Matching mortar is important when repointing deteriorated mortar joints in historic brick or stone piers.

The major damage to porches is caused by water, insects, and the settling that naturally occurs over time. The course of normal wear and tear may simply bring materials to the end of their usefulness. In other instances, a change in use—for example, enclosing the porch—may add stress that cannot be tolerated by the historic materials. These problems will often show up in the porch foundation, i.e., the piers and footings. The footings, if any, are often washed away when water runoff from the house or porch roof is not carried away from the house by a good drainage system (Fig. 118). It is important to keep water from collecting under the porch. This may be accomplished simply by sloping the ground away from the house and covering the area with a waterproof barrier such as plastic sheeting and a layer of gravel. Also effective is a small, gravel-filled trench with small, perforated drains placed about a foot outside of the perimeter of the porch and buried below the surface (see Fig. 112). Either method, when coupled with a porch apron that allows ventilation under the porch, should discourage water from collecting.

Measures to prevent water damage to the substructure include the use of preservatives, water repellents, and rot-resistant species of wood. Any new wood member used for replacement, if it is to be in contact with the ground, should be pressure-treated to discourage mildew or decay fungi (dry rot) not to mention insects. Rot-resistant soft woods, such as Western red cedar, redwood, cypress, and, to a lesser extent, Douglas fir, are less vulnerable to fungal and insect attacks. Untreated, they are more effective in above-ground applications such as joists, railings, and stair parts. Parts of the existing porch that are still sound may be treated with water-repellent preservatives that protect against mold and mildew and, in some cases, from decay and insects. Preservative treatment is necessary whenever wood is in contact with the soil.

Insect damage is identifiable by small holes bored in wooden members (Fig. 119), or shelter tubes (Fig. 120) built on the surfaces leading from

MORTAR

Historically, masonry work on porches was restricted to the foundation of the house and the piers supporting the porch. Brick piers were constructed with a soft mortar composed mainly of sand. When repointing historic masonry, it is important to mix a mortar that is strong enough to be compatible with the old, soft bricks, yet elastic enough to prevent spalling when the bricks expand and contract.

Another aspect of repointing historic masonry is the appearance of the masonry joint, or the joint profile. Profiles vary from concave to convex; they may be beaded, or V-jointed, or flush (Fig. 116). Before attempting to repoint the joint, a few test patches of mortar should be mixed and allowed to dry to verify the color and consistency of the dried mortar. Stonework, when exposed on a porch, often displays a bead of different color mortar. This practice is known as "tuckpoint-

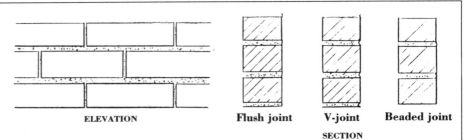

ELEVATION **Flush joint** **V-joint** **Beaded joint**

SECTION

Figure 116. The masonry joint may be finished in a variety of styles: flush joints vary in thickness from butter-thin to one-half inch typically; beaded joints are highly decorative but tend to wear faster than flush joints; and V-joints will wear at the ends and may cause the corners of the brick or stone to deteriorate.

ing (Fig. 117). Tuckpointing is generally found on high-style porches. This detail requires quite a bit of skill in preparing the bed mortar (i.e., the first layer of mortar) for the decorative colored mortar bead. A skilled mason should be contracted to perform this masonry work, with careful supervision by the owner to ensure the quality of work.

Figure 117. Tuckpointing is the insertion of a colored bead of mortar in the mortar bed.

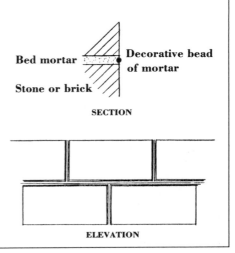

Bed mortar **Decorative bead of mortar**
Stone or brick

SECTION

ELEVATION

Figure 118. Faulty gutters have resulted in a washed-out foundation. The earth surrounding the pier footings has eroded, removing their support. This problem could have been prevented by installing gutters and providing the proper foundation drainage.

Figure 119. Wooden piers are susceptible to insect damage as illustrated here. The replacement piers should have been treated with wood preservative to prevent insect infestation.

Figure 120. Typical termite shelter tubes.

Wall of the house

Porch floor

Ledger board

Flashing

Figure 121. A small piece of continuous metal flashing installed between the wall of the house and the ledger board. The flashing should be bent to be parallel to the ground.

wooden members to the ground. Termites thrive in moist areas; damp wood will almost always reveal white "worker" termites wandering around. A licensed exterminator should treat the soil and regularly inspect the foundation. Any cracks in the foundation, often hidden by the porch, can become passages for termites to the house itself, and should be identified and sealed. Another way to discourage insects is to create a physical barrier such as "termite flashing." These strips of metal at all joints between the piers and the wood structure or the house foundation and the ledge supporting the porch will prevent the insects from reaching the wood (Fig. 121).

The only way to discover any of the symptoms of rot or insect damage in the early stages is to crawl under the porch and inspect each component. This should be done with caution, as the damage to the structural members may be extensive, and indiscriminate prodding of fragile piers could result in an accident. If there is any doubt about the security of a support, take the time to insert some precautionary shoring. Also bear in mind that skunks, snakes, bats, and the like enjoy damp, dark places such as the undersides of porches.

Check to see whether the porch floor is level. The porch may slope to one side or one of the posts may be slightly off-center. Good porch design includes a slope of one-quarter inch per foot away from the house to allow for water drainage. Sloping that runs across the house, however, is probably due to uneven settling of the ground around the footings. This creates stress on all the other parts of the structure, resulting in leaning posts, cracked footings and piers, and, in severe cases, collapse. Make a note to check the footings and piers if the porch is obviously not level (Fig. 122).

Wooden supports are more susceptible to water damage than brick or masonry piers. Because wood posts were usually set in the ground, the end grain, the most vulnerable and absorbent part of the wood, was in direct contact with the moist soil; few if any porches of this type have survived. If you wish to retain existing wooden porch piers, it is advisable to install a concrete base with a stirrup of galvanized metal set in its center. This stirrup will hold either an existing wood support or a new support made of pressure-treated lumber and allow water to drain away from the post (Fig. 123).

If the porch pier has to be replaced, consider installing a footing if none exists. In order to pour a new footing, the ground should be excavated at the site of the old post and the footing forms constructed in a dimension calculated for your porch. As a rule of thumb, the footing should be the width of the support multiplied by two, with a depth of six inches below the frost line ending in a larger slab twelve inches deep (Fig. 124). Another option is to install a sonotube footing. This is a preformed tube of heavy-

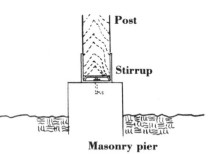

Figure 122. A leaning porch post may indicate settling around one of the footings or a water runoff problem. Try to evaluate the entire structure for all possible causes before beginning to correct the symptoms.

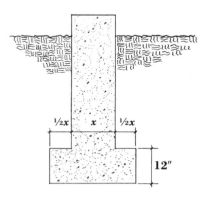

Figure 123. A new wood porch support should be installed with a post stirrup to allow the water to drain away from the post end.

duty cardboard inserted into the ground and filled with concrete. The cardboard eventually deteriorates, leaving the concrete form intact.

Masonry piers should be free from cracks, split stones or blocks, or spalled brick. Spalling results from the freezing and thawing cycle after water infiltrates a masonry wall through a deteriorated mortar joint; it may be evident in cracked brick, exfoliation of the stone (where the stone appears to be "peeling"), or overall failure of the brick. Masonry joints should be periodically inspected for deterioration (Fig. 125). Any missing or damaged joints must be repointed with a mortar compound of similar strength and composition to match the historic material.

Check to see if the porch floor is resting evenly on its supports. There should be no gaps, however slight, between the beam supporting the floor joists and the piers. Before making any repairs, try to determine the source of the damage. If one pier has settled, the porch can be jacked up until it is level and the settled pier then built up. One pier may have moved and caused additional stress on another footing. It would be useless to repair the second footing without knowing why the first pier moved. It may be that the footing of the first pier has begun to wash out from the runoff of rain water at the base of the porch (see Fig. 118).

Inspect the header beam supporting the floor joists. Has it been damaged by rot or weathering, insects, or old age? It may not be necessary to replace the entire member. If only a small area has been damaged, especially at the ends, a new piece of lumber can be bolted onto the old one, or a new member can be strapped to the original with metal braces, a process known as "sistering" (Fig. 126). Floor joists, the intermediary

Figure 124. The support pier should be centered in a footing that is twice as wide as the pier and approximately one foot high. The overall depth of the support pier and footing is determined by the local building code and is based on local climatic conditions.

Figure 125. Masonry exhibits many signs of water infiltration, including the joint deterioration displayed here. One joint may have deteriorated and the subsequent freeze-thaw cycle caused the remaining joints to pop.

structural members supporting the porch floor, suffer from the same afflictions as the header boards. Also check the ledger board supporting the porch on the house foundation wall. It is especially prone to insect damage, as well as damage from water running down the exterior wall of the house. The wood, if sound, should be treated with a preservative, flashed to prevent insect damage, and caulked at the top joint to prevent water damage.

While you are under the porch, check the condition of the floorboards. Water drainage problems will be indicated by dark, damp wood. Make a note to discover why a wet spot is occurring in that area—perhaps a leaky roof or a low spot in an uneven floor allowed water to collect. These damaged boards will probably have to be replaced. In some cases, however, only the ends are damaged; those boards might be salvaged with epoxies (Fig. 127). Also note the condition of the porch apron and fascia trim, if it still remains. Most often the apron is the first item to deteriorate. This is probably due to its proximity to the damp ground, and the tendency

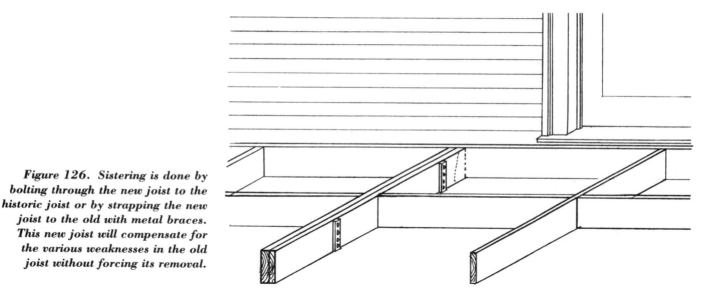

Figure 126. Sistering is done by bolting through the new joist to the historic joist or by strapping the new joist to the old with metal braces. This new joist will compensate for the various weaknesses in the old joist without forcing its removal.

Figure 127. Floorboards that display only end damage are candidates for epoxy restoration.

EPOXIES

Epoxies are useful when you want to restore rotted woodwork but don't possess the skills to splice it or don't want to go to the expense of having the old materials replicated (Fig. 128).

Epoxies are not, however, miracle workers. Consider their conditions and limits before you decide to use them. Epoxies will be useful if the decorative molding or architectural element would otherwise be too costly or inconvenient to replace or repair conventionally. But epoxies work best when the finished surface is to be covered with a coat of paint; a wood patch is better for unpainted surfaces. Another disadvantage of epoxies is that, while they can take some compression, they cannot tolerate tensile force as well and therefore should not be used in joists, beams, or other structural members without adequate reinforcement. Their use in structural areas is even more dangerous in case of fire, where they will tend to melt even before timber ignites. After a fire, an epoxy-repaired wooden member may appear sound until weight is applied and the epoxy gives way. In general, epoxies work well on floorboard ends, column bases and capitals, balustrades and railings, trims, moldings, windowsills, etc., if there is enough wood fiber to consolidate and if the area is small.

Figure 128. Epoxies can be used to repair the delicate trim even in this condition. A liquid epoxy will be necessary to consolidate the damage and a high-viscosity paste will fill in the voids.

Epoxies generally require a two-part process: a consolidant, or a low-viscosity liquid, which seeps into and consolidates the deteriorated area; and a patching compound, a high-viscosity paste, which fills the voids. Once set, epoxy can be planed or sanded. The consolidant is necessary when the patch area is rotted but may be skipped if the wood is in good condition. Finish with a coating of wood preservative and paint. It is important to remember that the consolidant works only on the end grain of the wood; it may be necessary to drill holes into the deteriorated area to reach all the affected wood.

Epoxies are volatile and poisonous materials. Follow all instructions concerning ventilation, mixing, and disposal. Epoxies give off a great deal of heat as they cure, which may cause damage to the piece you intend to fix and may even be a fire hazard when working with old, dried-out wood.

of rain water to splash back onto the lattice. Other problems are created when foundation plantings are placed too close to the porch. A good rule of thumb is to plant bushes at least two to three feet away from the porch and trim them periodically. If the porch apron and trim are not salvageable, but the design is original to the porch, you may want to use them as a pattern for the replacement.

Floors

In old porches, the major problems come from exposure and water damage. No surface is more vulnerable to these afflictions than the floor of the porch. Its condition usually reflects both the condition of the substructure and the condition of the roof. The floorboards, especially after the 1800s, are commonly jointed in a tongue-in-groove manner (Fig. 129). The porch

Figure 129. The tongue-in-groove flooring that is commonly found on Victorian-style porches is a stock lumberyard item.

Figure 130. A Colonial porch entry would have half-lapped joints (as shown here) or butt joints. In either case, the planks would be of varying widths.

floor should rest directly on the floor joists of the substructure, but wood tends to shrink over time, causing the boards to separate. In addition, the age-old expansion-contraction cycle will cause buckling and warping, further separating the boards. If in good condition, these original boards may be carefully renailed in position after you clean out the "grooves" of the tongue-in-groove to remove all the old putty and dirt. Reinstall to allow for expansion and contraction, as discussed below.

When replacing a part of the old flooring with new, make sure that the new wood is compatible with the old both in species and joint type. Otherwise the boards will expand and contract at different rates, causing more stress in the wood. When replacing the entire floor of a Victorian porch, it is best to use a tongue-in-groove three-inch-by-five-quarter dimension, which is a stock lumberyard item. A Colonial porch, however, would have originally had a half-lapped plank floor with planks of varying widths (Fig. 130); this can be ordered at a lumberyard with access to a mill. The wood should be Douglas fir if possible, as it is one of the hardest softwoods with a dense, close grain commonly available at the lumberyard. Woods such as pine and cedar are not a good choice for flooring; they are too soft and wear poorly. Treat all floorboards with a preservative, preferably before installation, to coat both the exposed side and the underside of the floor. When laying the floor, place the boards perpendicular to the house. The porch floor should slope one-quarter inch per foot away from the house. Set a one-eighth-inch expansion joint between the house and the floor. This gap may be caulked and covered with a finished nosing in a style appropriate to the age of the porch (see Bibliography for pattern books that include molding and wood detail profiles). Another expansion joint, one-sixteenth every four boards, should be included to provide for expansion across the floor. Caulk each floorboard on the "tongue" side of the board before nailing in at each joist. Sand the floor to a smooth surface and apply a new coat of preservative, giving special attention to sanded areas and freshly cut ends of the floorboards, before painting.

Porch floors will last about as long as any other feature of the porch if properly maintained. The ends of the porch floor require particular attention since that is where the spongelike end grain is exposed. A curved nosing should be routed on the straight edge of the floor, to minimize the amount of end grain and create a finished appearance. The plantings surrounding a porch should be kept trimmed back to prevent water from dripping onto the ends and to increase air circulation. A porch floor should also stop short of the roof overhang for the same reason.

Stairs

Like porch supports, porch stairs are in close contact with the ground, and, along with the newel posts, are equally susceptible to rot and decay. Repair of these components is inevitable, but before you replace them, study them carefully. Replace the historic materials, when necessary, with like materials. Wood stairs, for example, are in keeping with a wood porch—a concrete stair and iron railings are not.

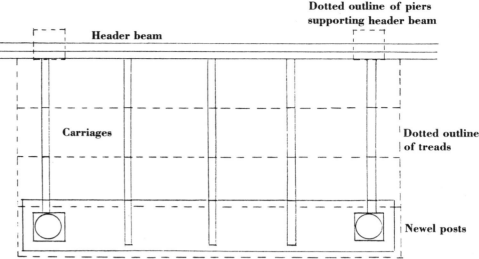

Header beam

Dotted outline of piers
supporting header beam

Carriages

Dotted outline
of treads

Newel posts

Figure 131. This framing plan for the stairs illustrates the newel posts cut into the first stair tread. The stair carriages and newel posts are anchored with post anchors in the concrete.

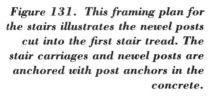

Stair carriage

Anchor

Footing

Figure 132. The carriages are set in metal anchors to prevent contact with the ground.

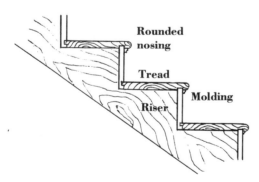

Rounded
nosing

Tread

Molding

Riser

Figure 133. The finish details of a well-built stair. The rabetted joint between the tread and riser prevents the cupping of the treads and reinforces the nailed connection. The tread overhangs the riser by one inch, with a rounded nosing routed on the end. The molding covers the joint between the tread and riser and completes the finish detail.

Newel posts can be restored in much the same manner as porch posts (see the section on porch posts). If only the top of the newel post is damaged, you can use epoxies for repair; if the base is deteriorated (a more likely occurrence), a new base can be spliced.

If posts are missing or beyond restoration, replacements can be found at the many companies that carry replicas of newel posts as stock items, or at an architectural salvage yard (check the yellow pages and the Sources of Supply section at the back of this book). You should be able to select one in keeping with the style of your porch. To match the original exactly, go to a mill that does custom turning. Once chosen, the newel posts are best secured with the same galvanized post anchors used for the porch posts. Set the ground level anchors for the newel posts in concrete (Fig. 131). The post anchors are covered when the posts are incorporated into the stair. If the posts were designed to be exposed, use a piece of trim to cover the exposed metal.

Porch stairs are relatively easy to restore and maintain if they are designed correctly. Stairs are composed of the carriage, treads, and risers. When these three components must be replaced, always use preservative-treated lumber. As with newel posts, set the carriages in galvanized metal anchors secured in a concrete slab, to prevent the exposed end grain from touching the ground (Fig. 132). The carriage design should also incorporate a slope of one-eighth inch on each tread, with the treads themselves designed to project an inch over the edge of the riser. The treads should be made from a hard, densely grained softwood such as Douglas fir. Finish this projecting edge with a rounded nosing (Fig. 133).

Ventilation is the best preservative for the underside of the porch steps. A lattice or other open-work apron will allow the air to circulate underneath the stairs and prevent the moisture from accumulating (Fig. 134).

Railings

The porch railings are comprised of a top railing, a base rail, and balusters or pickets. They have many flat surfaces that hold moisture and ornate turnings that tend to wear poorly. The top rail is often built up from multiple pieces of molding and blocking, leaving a small channel for installation of a fillet to space the balusters. The top of the rail is usually covered with a cap that is sloped to drain off water. The base rail is usually a single piece of wood, also shaped to drain moisture. The baluster, or picket, is secured either by toe-nailing the picket in place or by using a fillet, or blocking, to space the pickets properly. The fillet piece would be screwed into place with the screws countersunk and filled (Figs. 135, 136).

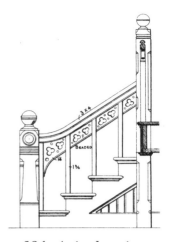

Figure 134. A simple stair apron, like the one shown, allows the air to circulate under the porch steps.

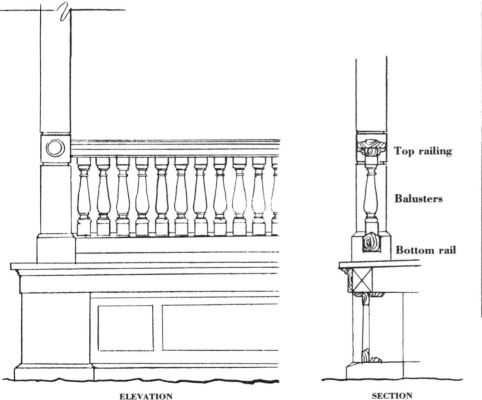

ELEVATION   SECTION

Top railing

Balusters

Bottom rail

Figure 135. These drawings are of sections cut through a typical balustrade. Note that the bottom rail is one piece while the top rail is made up of many pieces. Balusters and railing systems vary from ornate turned urns to simple groupings of pickets. In all cases, the bottom rail and top railing must be shaped to drain water. The design of the balusters should also minimize horizontal surfaces, which hold moisture.

Figure 136. In the less common sawn railing system, the two-dimensional rail was made from a sawn board.

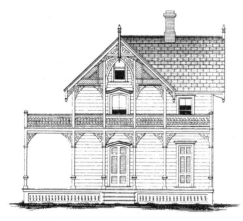

Figure 137. This cutout pattern is made up of slats with repeating simple geometric cuts on the edges of the boards.

Aprons

Porch aprons are at once functional and beautiful. Their primary purposes are to screen the unbecoming substructure of the porch and prevent small unwelcome creatures from taking up residence in the crawl space. At the same time, they allow air to circulate and ventilate the underside of the porch, helping water to evaporate.

Due to the proximity of the apron to the ground, it is often the area most susceptible to water damage. Over the years, the ground tends to build up around the apron, sometimes embedding the bottom rail of the apron frame. This would cause the apron to eventually rot away and, too often, be replaced by an inappropriate substitute. If this is true of your house, it is worthwhile to take the time to research what might have been there. If no old photos exist, you can still design and construct a replacement that is sensitive to the architecture of the house and porch.

Whether replacing the porch apron or simply repairing it, consider regrading the area around the porch to create a two- to three-inch minimum clearance between the rail of the apron frame and the ground. If you're replacing the apron, it might be convenient to incorporate a hinged access door in a side panel. This will create an outdoor storage area.

Historically, two types of porch aprons were popular. The first type, typically of the Italianate and Gothic period, was a two-dimensional sawn pattern, repeating ornate geometric cutouts (Fig. 137). If the porch has an existing apron of this type, use one of the pieces as a template. (It is important to remove the paint buildup first, because the layers of paint distort the pattern.) The sawn pieces are attached to a picture frame through either toe-nailing the slats flush with the frame or securing the slats behind the frame (Fig. 138).

Figure 138. This is a section through the sawn-pattern porch apron. In this example, the slats are secured by screwing them through to the frame (usually a 2" × 4"). The finished frame is then installed over the secured slats.

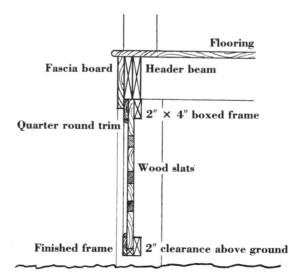

Flooring

Fascia board
Header beam

2" × 4" boxed frame

Quarter round trim

Wood slats

Finished frame
2" clearance above ground

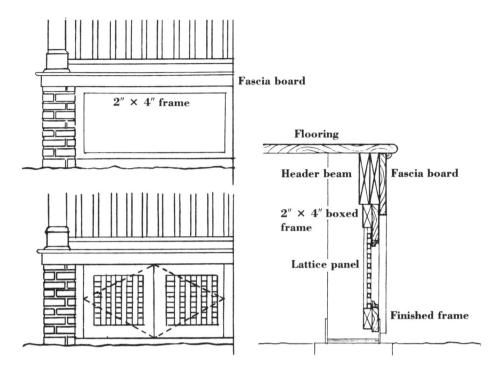

Fascia board

2" × 4" frame

Flooring

Header beam

Fascia board

2" × 4" boxed
frame

Lattice panel

Finished frame

Figure 139 (far left). The support-
ing frame of the lattice should box
out the area between the piers. This
will provide support for the lattice
and finished frame. The access door
should open out to allow maximum
entry to the underside of the porch.
The support frame will brace the
door and secure the hinges.

Figure 140 (left). This section
through the lattice panel shows how
the lattice is secured directly to the
frame and then the finished frame is
installed over the panel.

The second type of porch apron, found in later architectural styles, is lattice. Constructed of soft wood, it tends to wear rapidly unless it was built and maintained well. To reconstruct a lattice porch apron, select pressure-treated wood for the frame. The picture-frame molding should be clear pine treated with preservative. Lattice purchased from a lumber-yard will be a standard size of $\frac{5}{16}$" x 1½" x 48", smaller than the typical historic custom-milled lattice strips. All lattice pieces should be dipped in a wood preservative and allowed to dry. Brush a prime coat on *all* sides of the lattice and paint two top coats *before* the lattice is nailed in place.

While waiting for the strips to dry, frame out the enclosure, allowing for an access door. The access door should have heavy-duty hinges and proper bracing (Fig. 139).

Once it is framed, nail the lattice into place, the top layer over the back layer. Staples are not recommended as they tend to rust and wear poorly. If you are putting in a large amount of lattice, it is useful to set up a framing pattern box to ensure that all the slats are square when nailed in place. In addition, if covering a long span of open framework, insert bracing behind the lattice and secure it to the frame. Backset the nails and fill the nail holes with putty (Fig. 140).

In an area where the lattice will receive a lot of wear and tear—an urban sidewalk porch, for example—it may be worthwhile to construct heavy-duty lattice, which means using a full 1" x 1" picket stock lumber, routing the top and bottom layers a half inch at every joint or "cross," and securing with wood screws at every joint (Fig. 141). The lattice is then attached to a frame. This is a labor-intensive undertaking, but com-

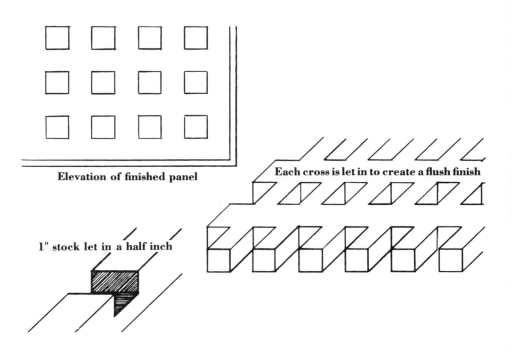

Figure 141. Heavy-duty lattice is made from picket stock lumber and "let in" at every cross to create a flush surface. The frame would then be secured over the edges of the panel.

Elevation of finished panel

Each cross is let in to create a flush finish

1″ stock let in a half inch

pared to replacing the "lighter" lattice every few years, it may pay for itself many times over.

A few words about prefabricated lattice: The pressure-treated lattice available at the lumberyard is not only sized differently than historic lattice, but it is generally more open, defeating one of its purposes, i.e., to keep small creatures out of the porch crawl space. If you do use the prefabricated, pressure-treated wood lattice, consider attaching a screen behind it. You will also need a frame to give the lattice a finished look. When you buy, verify that the pressure-treated lattice can be painted immediately. Depending on the method of treating the wood, it may be as much as a year until the wood is dry enough to paint.

A relatively new product is pvc or "plastic" lattice, which closely approximates the size of older lattice. It is difficult to tell the difference between wood and vinyl lattice when the wood is painted, and pvc can even be ordered in a wide variety of stock colors. But a common complaint about vinyl siding also plagues the new pvc lattice: in freezing weather they both become brittle and crack.

Columns

The main source of deterioration in columns is water damage and, subsequently, rot. The signs of rot and its effects vary, depending on the type of column and the way it was put together.

There are primarily three types of columns: solid, hollow, and laminate. Within these types are subtypes; a solid column, for example, may have been cut from the center of a tree trunk, in which case the heart of the tree runs its center, or from an area beside the heart, which would then not be visible. A column with a heart in the center is more prone to cracks or checks because as it dries, it shrinks.

The hollow column can be made from a solid blank that has its center bored out, relieving the stresses caused by drying and reducing the tendency to check. A hollow column may also be made up of staves glued together at the joints to form the shaft. The staves interlock in a variety of joint styles. Although the staved column is the most stable type of column there is, a primary problem is a failure at the glued joints which results in stave separation (Fig. 142).

The last type, the laminate column, is constructed of common lumber, usually 2″x4″ boards glued together, then trimmed to the proper shape. It is generally considered the strongest of the three. Although failure can come from delamination (glue failure), laminated columns are often used where a stronger shaft is necessary. Make certain to replace this kind of column with one of equal strength.

Inspecting the columns should reveal both the type of column and any impending problems. Peeling paint is an indication that there is a lot of moisture in the wood. Moisture accelerates the decay cycle (see Chapter 15) and deteriorates the glue in the joints. Extremes of wet and dry also cause stresses in the wood as it expands and shrinks, resulting in sprung staves in hollow columns and checks in solid and bored columns. Sprung staves are often also a result of uneven loading. If two or more staves in a row are sprung, check for uneven loading above and below the column. Repair of a column requires removing it from the porch. First, properly jack the porch roof up off the columns (see Chapter 17). Once the load is taken off the column, the base can be removed and the shaft can be dropped down and pulled away.

Column repair should be performed by a skilled carpenter. For all the strength of a column, it is constructed to carry a compressive load; it will not tolerate stresses applied to its individual parts. For example, repairing sprung staves requires proper tools and patience. The stave must be gently pushed back into alignment with its neighbors. First, place a block cut to the shape of the inside of the staves at each end of the column, attaching the block to adjacent sections of the sprung stave. Place a band clamp over the highest part of the sprung stave, with a wood block between the clamp head and the stave. Using the clamp, gently push the stave back into alignment. Fasten it into place with blocks of wood placed at different intervals on the inside of the column. These blocks should be screwed to each neighboring stave and twice again on the repaired stave. The screws should be countersunk and the holes filled with exterior filler (Fig. 143).

If the staves have separated at the joints due to glue failure, the column

Figure 142. There are two hollow types of columns. A staved column is made up of slats or staves that are "locked" together with different joint types or simply glued together. A bored column is made from a solid blank that is then hollowed out.

A solid column has three types: a column cut from the center of a tree, from the area beside the heart, or laminated from multiple pieces of lumber that are then finished to the proper shape.

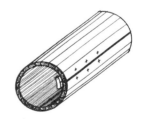

Figure 143. This is an exaggerated example of the stave separation. The wood blocks are cut to the interior profile of the column and screwed into place at multiple intervals (as indicated by the crosses). All of these screw holes will be countersunk and filled with putty.

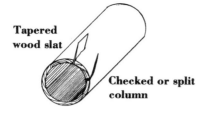

Tapered
wood slat

Checked or split
column

Figure 144. One method to repair slight checks or stave separation is to install a tapered slat, which is glued on one side and caulked on another. At its widest point, the slat must be wider than the gap you intend to fill. Leave some of the slat outside of the column surface until the glue has set, then trim the excess and sand the surface smooth.

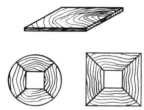

Figure 145. Base problems are often a result of their manufacture. The simple board base has two long sides of vulnerable and absorbent end grain. A revised design would decrease the amount of exposed end grain, in both the square and the round base.

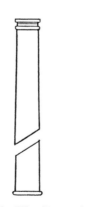

Figure 146. The base of the column shaft can be removed when deteriorated and a new base spliced onto the original column. Note the downward-sloping miter to create a positive moisture drain.

joints must be scraped free of all paint, caulk, dirt, old glue, etc., then glued with weatherproof glue and held with heavy band clamps. Glue one joint at a time until two opposite joints are left. These last two should be glued at the same time, following this procedure: Place the glue on either side of the joint and set in place. The joints should be clamped every twelve inches. Tighten the clamps a little at a time, forcing excess glue out of the joint. Calipers are recommended to check the roundness of the shaft. Allow two days for the joint to attain full strength before gluing the next joint.

Make sure that if only one joint is loose, the column has enough flexibility to close one joint without breaking another. If not, a wooden slat, glued on one side and caulked on another, tapered slightly and wider than the gap at its widest point, can be driven into the gap, leaving some of the slat outside of the surface. After the glue has set, trim off the excess glue and wood slat. This method can also be used to repair checks in a solid or bored column (Fig. 144).

The base of a column is usually where most of the rot occurs. Frequently, its problems are the result of the way it was manufactured. The base of the column was often made by cutting a single piece of wood and shaping it, rather than using several pieces of wood to form a base with minimal end-grain exposure. As with solid columns, the drying and aging process causes the wood to check and split because most of the exposed area is the vulnerable end grain. End grain is more likely than side grain to check and also acts as a sponge, allowing water to seep in and be drawn up inside the column (Fig 145).

In some cases, the rotted wood may be confined to the lower portion of the shaft and/or the base of the column, so only a portion of the column needs to be redone. The shaft end may be replaced by matching the wood species, the direction of the grain, and the column construction type. If splicing the lumber, do so with a downward-sloping miter to prevent trapping moisture. The new base should be composed of segments made up mostly of side grain and very little end grain. Keep joints to the minimum, however, because they are subject to the same glue failure as the staved column (Fig. 146).

The primary defense against deterioration is a paint film, which prevents water from seeping into the wood yet is permeable enough to allow the moisture trapped inside the column to escape. Paint that is too thick does not allow the water vapor to evaporate and results in blistering and peeling. If you have peeling or any scrapes or scratches that break the continuous film, the column should be scraped down to bare wood. Treat the wood with a preservative, prime with alkyd primer, and finish with two coats of exterior paint.

Hollow columns must be vented at the top through the soffit or capital on the nonweathering side (the one under cover), and screened if necessary to keep birds or insects out. Solid capitals can be protected by a flashing cap (Fig. 147).

When replacing the base or the plinth of a column, it is important to remember the slope of the porch floor. If the base or plinth is not leveled, the column cannot sit squarely and parts will be overstressed. The base should also be raised slightly above the porch floor to allow air to circulate underneath. This can be done with post anchors or stirrups of galvanized metal to anchor the column to the floor. The exposed metal ends of the stirrups can be hidden by a piece of trim around the plinth and must be caulked at all seams (Fig. 148).

Posts

Porch posts, like columns, are of three separate types: open, boxed, or solid. These types may be further divided into subtypes based on their method of construction. Open posts, for instance, may be either assembled or sawn from a single piece of wood. Boxed posts could be chamfered and/or routed, or built up further with geometric wood strips and curvilinear profile moldings. Solid posts could have been turned on a lathe or beveled at the corners (Figs. 149, 150, 151).

The signs of deterioration vary, but compared to columns, there are fewer glued joints and structural components to be damaged. Boxed posts, for example, are composed of four pieces of lumber forming the box. Repairs to this simple structural form, while major, can retain much of the original fabric by the simple use of nails, hammer, and some reinforcing plywood behind the original lumber. The applied decorative wood cutouts can be removed, if damaged, copied in the local lumberyard, and nailed back into place.

Solid posts are less easily repaired; however, the entire post need not be replaced if, say, only a portion at the base is rotten. A replacement section must be spliced into place, a reliable method as long as the original post has been dried and treated with a wood preservative to prevent spreading rot into the good lumber. If a solid post is too badly damaged to repair, a lumberyard can replicate it using the original as a template. When duplicating any damaged material, we warn you again to be careful to allow for the thickness of the old paint, as the addition of a one-quarter-inch paint layer can create a far different profile than you originally intended.

Open posts require quite a bit of maintenance since a good deal of end-grain wood is exposed. Checks form and allow moisture to seep in and rot to start. Splicing is difficult, especially if the sawn design is

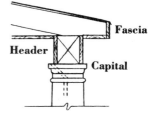

Dotted line indicates the line of ventilation

Figure 147. Hollow columns may be vented in two different ways: at top, venting on the nonweathering side of the column capital with a small screened vent, or (immediately above) raising the roof header slightly above the capital to allow air to circulate through the shaft.

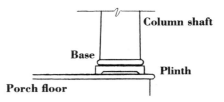

Figure 148. The base is slightly elevated above the porch floor and leveled to accommodate the slight pitch of the porch floor.

Figure 149. *An open post may be assembled from pieces as shown in the drawing of the lattice post or sawn from a single piece of wood as shown in the photograph.*

Figure 150. *A solid post could be simply chamfered as shown and dressed up at the base with fancy moldings. Another type of solid post is the later turned post as shown in the photograph.*

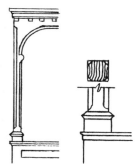

particularly ornate. If the open post is assembled from smaller pieces, the affected section can simply be removed and replaced.

Take the same preventative measures for posts as for columns (see the section on columns). Clean the wood of all old paint, putty, caulk, etc. Treat the posts with a preservative, prime, and finish with two coats of exterior latex or oil-base paint. Caulking at all joints is especially important at the base. Flashing and vent holes top and bottom are effective ways to circulate air and allow water vapor to escape. As with columns, the design of the base should include provisions for the slope of the porch.

Roof

The porch roof is the first line of defense in protecting the delicate trim and porch floor. The best way to anticipate—and ward off—problems is to examine the structural and water-shedding components (shingles, gutters, and flashings) for their solidity and integrity.

The structural components consist of the ledger beam, which connects the porch to the house, the rafters, and the beam that carries the rafters and is supported by the porch posts (Fig. 152). Water damage and rot are the chief destructive elements. If you find damage to the roof covering,

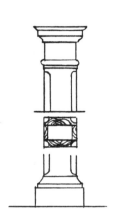

Figure 151. A boxed post is built up from multiple pieces that are then chamfered or dressed up with applied moldings.

Figure 152. Note that in Figs. 153, 154, 155, and 156 the structural components remain the same but were installed differently.

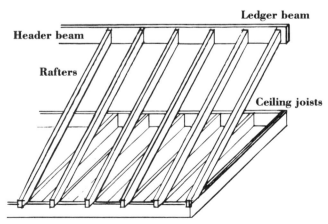

Header beam

Rafters

Ledger beam

Ceiling joists

Porch Maintenance and Repair **103**

Figure 153. Deteriorated sheathing under the roof covering must be replaced before replacing the roof.

examine the wood underneath it. Replace any damaged wood with preservative-treated lumber (Fig. 153).

Roof coverings vary with each style. Materials include sheet metal, wood or metal shingles, slate, and clay pantiles (Fig. 154). Canvas was also popular for a while. If you need to repair the covering, replace like with like. Remember the impact of the roof covering on the design and the structure. For example, covering a copper roof with an asphalt roofing compound will create a far different effect than the one originally intended. A change in the weight of the material used may also create other unexpected difficulties.

Wood shingles

Sheet-metal standing-seam roof

Clay pantile

Slate

Figure 154. Different roof coverings featured on different styles of architecture.

Figure 155. A simple hip-roof framing plan. The components act in the same manner as a simple shed roof, connecting at the house and carrying the load of the roof covering down to the header beam and posts, which then carry the weight to the ground. Note the hip rafter that interrupts the shed rafters, creating the distinctive profile. An alternate to this framing plan would be to nail the rafters flush with the inside of the header beam, instead of resting the rafters on top of the beam.

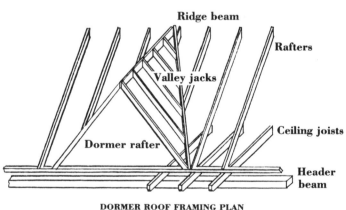

Figure 156. Many porch roof plans call for a small dormer over the entry stair.

As copper roofing has become more popular, kits are now available that include precut panels with prefolded seams. Copper is durable and resistant to corrosion by moisture. It may take eight to ten years to attain the natural green patina familiar on a historic house.

Wood shingles are another popular form of covering. Since they are susceptible to water damage, use a preservative. Wood shingles should be replaced when worn to one half their original thickness.

Slate is the most expensive material to replace and difficult for an amateur to install. It is, however, extremely durable if the job is done correctly. Consult a roofer if you are faced with the task of replacing an

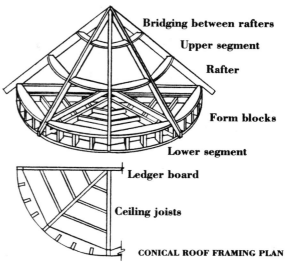

Figure 157. The conical roof frame.

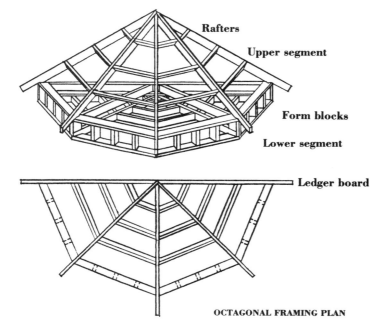

Figure 158. The octagonal framing plan is similar to the conical, including rafters, upper and lower segments, form blocks, and ceiling joists.

entire roof. There is a modern asphalt substrate that is indistinguishable at a distance from real slate.

Often the roof design is complex, requiring special flashing techniques. Flashing and counterflashing must be placed on anything protruding from the roof, including eaves, valleys, dormers, and cornices. It should extend seven to ten inches on either side of the valley protrusion. Take care in selecting flashing, as some metals, such as aluminum, may react chemically to their surroundings, by corroding, for example. Make sure when you purchase any roofing material that it will be compatible aesthetically and structurally with the existing roof (Figs. 155, 156, 157, 158).

15

What Causes Rot

Since most owners of old houses are constantly fighting a war against rot, it is beneficial to know the enemy. The cause of rot is decay fungi, but it can be one of several types and take several forms. *Bluestain* is usually identified by its dark color, blue, brown, gray, or black, and is caused by a fungus invading sapwood. By itself, it is not dangerous, but it often generates more damaging forms of rot. It is usually found around wood most exposed to water—the underside of a porch, in particular, or the porch supports. The spread of the color indicates the spread of decay as it carries water into the wood. Similarly, mold and mildew are relatively harmless, but make wood more susceptible to other forms of rot. They form a loose powdery mass of various rainbow colors on hardwood.

More dangerous forms of decay include *Brown Rot*, a brownish-colored fungus that eats away at cellulose, resulting in wood that cracks across the grain, then shrinks and loses strength rapidly. *White Rot* fungus, which causes wood to lose color and appear whitish, is deadly because it consumes both cellulose and lignin, causing the wood to become fibrous and stringy. Other than this whitish color change, there is no outward sign until the wood collapses. *Soft Rot* occurs only on surfaces, especially surfaces that are frequently wet (like your entire porch!); it causes severe cracks and fissures on surfaces both with and across the grain. Another form, "*dry rot*," is particularly dangerous because it can carry its own water supply as it spreads, thus creating an ideal environment for decay wherever it goes. It often spreads undetected until serious damage has occurred.

As mentioned previously, water is one of the four elements rot needs for growth. The others are oxygen, food (porch woodwork), and moderate temperature. Eliminate just one and you eliminate a favorable environment for rot. For example, to get rid of rot's food source, use a wood preservative to poison the fungus's environment. Wood preservatives, however, are poisonous to everything, so use caution in deciding when it will be applied and who shall be in contact with it.

Water is the most obvious culprit and possibly the most difficult link in the chain to eliminate. Sources include rain, snow, ground water, condensation in crawl spaces, and capillary action in the foundation wall, which carries water up to the ledger board. Rain attacks any exterior surface that has an open joint or seam not protected by a caulk or paint film. This inevitably includes porch rails, doors and window frames, and decorative trim. Gutters flood down into cornice and interior partitions, providing a moisture source for rot to attack rafter ends. Rain also penetrates through loose flashing, loose or missing shingles, and exposed nailheads. Warning signs of penetration include peeling, blistering paint on the underside of the soffit.

There are many immediate measures you can take to prevent water damage. Ground-level solutions include: sloping the ground away from the house, covering the ground directly under the porch with polyethylene sheets topped with gravel, ringing the perimeter with perforated drains in a gravel trunk, and increasing air circulation by installing a lattice porch apron. Make sure any wood that is not pressure-treated clears the ground by eight inches. Never plant vegetation close to the foundation.

The accumulation of moisture in the roof structure can be prevented by providing eaves' flashing to prevent ice dams, installing adequate gutters, and replacing shingles as needed. Make sure that the roofing nails are flush with the roof and adequately protected by overlapping material.

Most of the other elements of the porch, including the ornamental rails and trim, floors and stairs, can be protected with paint. Once that film or coating is broken, water seeps in, causing blistering and peeling and further accelerating the water seepage. Through normal wear and tear, the paint surface will inevitably scratch and crack, so the wood should be further protected with water repellents and preservatives (see Chapters 17 and 18). Stain, often used on Victorian porches, also provides a protective surface because it contains preservatives and water repellents.

Yearly inspection is especially useful in detecting rot before it does major damage. When you suspect rot, the pick test will determine the condition of the wood. An awl or ice pick jabbed into a piece of wood (in an inconspicuous place!) preferably while the wood is wet, will produce long splinters if the wood is healthy. Rotted wood produces short sections breaking across the grain without creating splinters.

If you discover rot, the first thing to do is to eliminate the source of moisture, arresting the spread of the superficial rot. Replace wood that is materially weakened; nonstructural wood (trim, rails, etc.), however, may be restored with epoxy materials. Bear in mind that any infected wood left in place will contaminate healthy wood if moisture is introduced. Finally, treat the new wood with preservatives, especially at joints and cracks. It is a good practice to give all exterior wood surfaces a coat of preservative every two years. Then caulk and putty to plug holes and cracks.

16

How Water Attacks the Porch

To protect the surface of the wood, it is essential to know where water typically collects, as well as the signs of water accumulation. Step back and study the porch; decay often begins at construction joints and the vulnerable exposed end grains.

Horizontal surfaces such as the floor shed water slowly. Vertical surfaces, on the other hand, are prone to uncontrolled runoff and splash-backs where soil is in close contact with the wood.

Here are some simple corrective measures you can take:

1. Install gutters and flashing to draw runoff away from the wood. Historically, hanging gutters were not used on porches; the Yankee gutters that were used quickly deteriorated if they were not well maintained. If you do install a gutter, do it sensitively. Downspouts should be located on side elevations where possible and the gutters painted to blend in with the porch trim (Figs. 160, 161).

2. Regrade or redesign surrounding areas to prevent splash-back from the ground, and remove soil in contact with the structure or trim. Add a thin layer of gravel at the perimeter of the porch, for example. This will "catch" the runoff and prevent splash-back.

3. Paint, caulk, and seal joints and seams. Dip or brush bare joints with a water repellent and caulk, and maintain a paint film at joints at all times.

4. The use of pressure-treated new lumber for any lumber in contact with the soil and the use of water repellents on existing lumber will retard the decay process. (Be sure to follow precautions suggested by manufacturer when working with pressure-treated lumber.)

PREVENTATIVE MAINTENANCE

Once the porch is in tip-top shape, an annual inspection should be made to determine whether any further preventative medicine is required. Reassure yourself that the porch roof is draining properly and that there are no loose or damaged shingles or slates, the gutters are not blocked, and the leaders are taking water away from the porch. Any flat areas, like the floor and some styles of trim and railings, should be inspected to ensure that the paint film, wood's first line of defense, is not peeling or scratched.

The substructure, once restored or rebuilt, should last for years. However, try to have it inspected once a year for termites and other wood-boring insects. It may be advisable to set up a routine treatment schedule with a professional exterminator (Fig. 159).

Figure 159. Seasonal inspections should pay particular attention to the following areas:

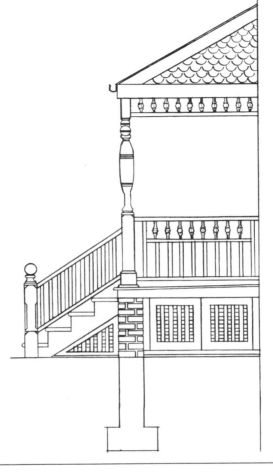

ROOF: Make sure that all the material is secure and that the flashing is still intact.

GUTTERS AND DOWNSPOUTS: Make sure these are free from debris like leaves, acorns, etc. Check the fascia behind the gutter for indications of water damage. Make sure this paint film is intact.

CEILING: Investigate any areas of dampness. They could indicate failure of the roofing material or flashing.

POSTS: Make sure that the paint film on the post bases or column base and plinth is intact. There should be no blistering paint.

PORCH FLOOR: Pay particular attention to the ends; rises in the flooring may indicate that water is sitting on the floor instead of draining.

SUBSTRUCTURE: Check the walls of the house as well as the joists, beams, and piers for water damage and insect activity.

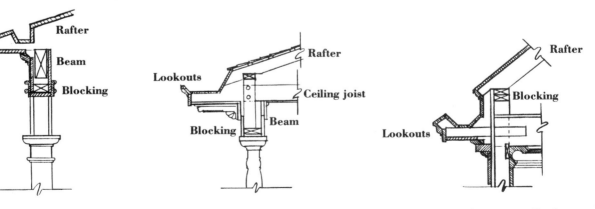

Figure 160. Gutters can be incorporated into the roof structure. Lookouts are tied back to the rafters or the ceiling joists, or the rafter tails are notched to accept a metal gutter lining. This method of construction hides the drainage system.

Figure 161. These photographs illustrate how water drainage systems might detract from the overall finished appearance of the porch. A more sensitive approach would be to install the gutters only where necessary, hidden up at the fascia board, painted to match if possible. The leaders could have been installed around the corner from the main elevation or behind the post, or attached to the side of the house.

17

Jacking Up a One-Story Porch

Upon inspection, you may have found numerous structural problems in the masonry piers or the porch columns. If these problems occur in several places on the porch, the only practical way to treat them is to jack the porch roof up off the piers or columns. This can be done expensively with hydraulic jacks or screw jacks, or inexpensively with timbers and some intelligently applied force. Either way, there are a few rules that should be followed to prevent mishaps.

A one-story porch is attached to the house in three places. These attachments are compressive in nature; that is, the force of gravity is carrying the weight of the load downward, and the attachments can tolerate only a small amount of tensile (bending) stress before they break. Therefore, the roof should be jacked up only until the stresses in the posts or columns are relieved, about one-quarter inch. Exceeding that limit will create stress on the ceiling joint and cause the porch roof to separate from the house (Fig. 162).

Another all-important rule to remember is that once the weight is lifted off the columns and posts, they are more likely to shift horizontally. If necessary, and especially if you are removing any of the rails for repair work, brace these columns or posts with purlins (horizontal bracing members) that reach from one column to another.

The process for taking the weight off the posts or columns with shoring timbers is simple. Materials include one 4″ x 6″ pine shoring timber per column, notched at one end to receive the roof load, plus one 2″ x 6″ plank per timber about four feet long, and wedges to place between the timber and the plank. Have a small block ready to be nailed behind the wedge.

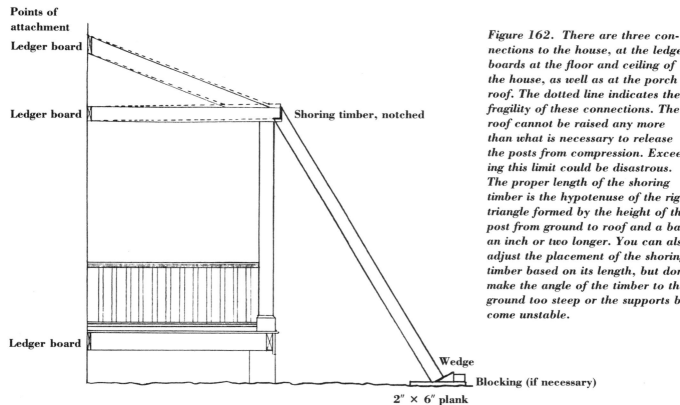

Points of attachment

Ledger board

Ledger board

Shoring timber, notched

Ledger board

Wedge

Blocking (if necessary)

2″ × 6″ plank

Figure 162. There are three connections to the house, at the ledger boards at the floor and ceiling of the house, as well as at the porch roof. The dotted line indicates the fragility of these connections. The roof cannot be raised any more than what is necessary to release the posts from compression. Exceeding this limit could be disastrous. The proper length of the shoring timber is the hypotenuse of the right triangle formed by the height of the post from ground to roof and a base an inch or two longer. You can also adjust the placement of the shoring timber based on its length, but don't make the angle of the timber to the ground too steep or the supports become unstable.

Working from one end of the porch, use a sledgehammer and the wedge to lift the porch roof off the columns and onto the timbers. Make sure there is enough rough surface to keep the plank under the timber from slipping. If not, a wider plank (3″ x 8″) should be used. When the columns are free, nail purlins between the shoring to prevent them from moving horizontally.

Once the roof load is removed, repair work to the posts or columns and the substructure is immediately accessible. Foundation work or work on the support piers is attained by using blocking or simple jacks to lift the sill beam off at any of the affected areas. Bear in mind, once again, the one-quarter-inch limit in order to avoid damaging any of the sill connections.

18

Painting the Porch

More so even than the physical labor, the most difficult aspect of painting your porch—and the most interesting—is choosing colors. Scraps of wood you have collected from restoring the porch can provide an accurate color history, but if you have no scraps to go by, or if the color of the main body of the house conflicts with the original porch color, you will have to do some research to find a color scheme appropriate to the history and style of the house.

There are a few simple rules to remember as you choose the colors. A house built in the Greek Revival era (1820–1845) would probably have been painted in "marble" colors: whites, pale pinks, beiges, or soft grays. The early Romantic-style cottage such as Italianate or Gothic (1843–1870) would have been a "stone" color: soft gray, green, tan, or pale ocher. The porch would be a shade lighter or darker than the body of the house, possibly a third color in delicate contrast to the color used on the house trim. The Queen Anne house (1870–1890), on the other hand, used "earth" colors: rich, dark greens, reds, browns, golds, and maroon. In this style, the porch is usually darker than the main body with trim, porch floors, and stair treads accented in a third, even stronger color. Colonial Revival houses (1890s and on) went back to white and pale colors and trimmed the porch in white. Arts and Crafts movement houses and bungalows returned to the dark stains of the Colonial period, with all trim painted in dark reds or browns (Figs. 163, 164, 165, 166).

Many excellent references on historic colors are available from the library and bookstores. Most of the major paint companies have developed a collection of historic paint colors, although often lacking the subtlety

Figure 163. Although the historic photographs here and in Figs. 164, 165, and 166 are black and white, it is possible to see how the various ornamental elements were differentiated by trim colors and darker shades of the overall porch color. This was done to achieve a sculptural effect, deepening shadow lines at overhangs and dentils, for example.

Figure 164. This photograph of part of the front porch illustrates again the use of various shades or colors to differentiate the trim from the lattice, or the base of the posts from the shaft of the posts.

Figure 165. A recent paint job on this historic porch reversed the traditional darker trim and lighter body. Note that the trim is done in the same color as the body of the house, tying the whole composition together.

and richness of the true nineteenth-century colors. Be careful to select a color that complements the architectural style of the porch.

There are a few general rules for applying color to the Victorian porch that may help you in determining a color scheme. First, there are few houses that warrant a three-color scheme, and extremely few, very ornate houses, that warrant more. A two-color scheme is usually the most successful for a porch: the color of the main body of the house, plus a contrasting color. Probably the most popular style is painting the main horizontal and vertical elements in the contrasting trim color, then using the color of the main body of the house to "punch out" the decorative elements within the posts or cornice. For example, paint the posts and the top and bottom rail in the same trim color as the corner boards or cornice of the house, and paint the pickets in the color of the main body of the house. Finish the porch cornice or fascia in the trim color used for the posts. If your porch roof is decorated with brackets that have recesses or panels, you could add the main body color to these recesses to show off the detail. Sometimes it is even possible to create the illusion of a shadow line within the framing of a panel by adding a bit of gray to the trim color.

Color schemes refuse to be tied down to one method, and you should consider the design of the porch before committing yourself to a color scheme. Sometimes the style of the balusters will determine the color for you. For example, ornate turned balusters resemble stone urns. The natural color choice: something from the stone family of grays, sandstone, or terra cotta. If you are fortunate enough to have a porch with ornate metalwork or cast-iron details, consider the lovely palette of weathered colors like bronze green or vandyke or verdigris.

The color of porch floors has historically been selected for practicality. Old photographs reveal that the floor was usually painted a dark color for the obvious reason that it did not show the dirt as readily. The famous battleship-gray color was popular for its availability and its durability. The floor was often a deeper tone (with more gray in it) than the contrasting trim color. This same principle held true for the porch steps: the tread was painted the dark color of the porch floor and the riser painted to match the body of the house.

The porch ceiling is another study in practicality. The porch often blocked the light coming into the main parlor of the house. One way to capture more light was to paint the underside of the ceiling in a bright color like white or robin's-egg blue. This is particularly true if the underside of the roof was left exposed instead of covered with a matchboard or wainscot ceiling. If the porch did have the matchboard ceiling, it may have been painted but was more likely oiled or varnished, retaining the natural appearance of the wood.

Preparing the surfaces to receive the paint is as important as selecting the correct colors. Good preparation will help to ensure a lasting paint finish, typically five years or more. If the paint surfaces on the porch have been well maintained, it may be necessary only to clean them with a mild detergent such as TSP (commonly available at hardware stores), and lightly scrape and sand the surface. Totally removing the mulitple layers of paint on the original woodwork is not recommended unless absolutely necessary. In many ways, the harsh methods used for paint stripping may permanently damage the historic woodwork.

The only case for removing the historic paint is when the paint surface displays deep cracks or extensive blistering and bare wood is exposed. But attack the problem cautiously. Methods like burning off the paint, sandblasting, or rotary sanders and wire strippers should be avoided. Even skilled craftsmen cannot control these tools well enough to ensure that woodwork will not be damaged.

The expedient methods, such as heat guns and orbital sanders, will create toxic dust and vapors from lead paint. It is important to take the recommended precautions, i.e., wearing respirators and goggles. Also check state or local environmental regulations when using any kind of paint stripper to find out how to best dispose of the effluent waste.

Figure 166. This house uses the more typical darker accent on the lighter body of the porch. It could have been made more ornate by detailing the leaves of the capitals with the trim color and creating shadow lines on the panel by painting the molding one tone darker than the body of the post.

Paint tends to fail where moisture problems are present, so don't bother to go through all the work to prepare and paint the surface unless you have successfully addressed the moisture problem. Even after you have done so, you may have to allow the wet surface to dry for an extended period of time before covering it with paint.

Another reason for paint failure is paint that has been built up too thickly. When this occurs, the paint closest to the wood tends to pull away from the wood surface. In addition, new paint has a much tighter adhesion than the historic paint, so as it dries, it "pulls" on the older paint and exacerbates the problem. Using an alkyd paint for the new layer may lessen the effect. Latex paint applied over oil-based paint will sometimes peel because the oil paint is less elastic than the latex paint when it dries.

When conditions such as peeling, crazed, or alligatored paint demand that the paint surface be stripped, the following methods are recommended:

- Abrasion or sanding, by manual or mechanical means such as scraping.
- Thermal stripping, by softening the paint surface with heat and scraping the loosened paint.
- Chemical stripping, by liquid or paste paint removers, loosening the paint adhesion to the wood or other surfaces for removal with scraping and sanding.

Methods you should not even consider:

- Waterblasting above six hundred pounds per square inch actually forces water into the woodwork, and high-pressure water-washing can penetrate the exterior sheathing and damage the interior finishes. Be aware that many chemical strippers require that the surface be washed down with a high-pressure water wash in order to ensure proper adhesion of the new paint finish. These brands of strippers should be avoided.
- Sandblasting, or any other type of abrasion by "blasting," should not be used on any historic fabric except cast iron. It erodes the wood fibers, leaving a pitted surface and in some cases will totally obliterate the moldings and delicate carvings.
- Blow-torching the paint surface should be avoided at all costs. If heat stripping is required, use a heat plate or heat gun. This will decrease the chance of setting the house on fire.

The importance of cleaning the surface properly before beginning to paint cannot be overemphasized. Airborne pollutants must be rinsed off all surfaces, particularly those surfaces not exposed to rainfall such as soffits.

Once the surfaces have been sanded and cleaned to remove all the residue from detergent and chalking, apply a high-quality primer compatible to the finish paint and allow it to dry thoroughly. An alkyd primer followed by a *high-gloss* oil-based paint is very successful in highlighting the details of the porch. Then inspect the porch for areas needing puttying or caulking. Fill these areas with a high-quality wood putty or resilient caulk and allow them to set per the manufacturer's recommendations. Once the areas have set, spot-prime the filled areas and allow them to dry. The finish coats (at least two) should be applied to the prepared surfaces and allowed to dry thoroughly between coats, according to the manufacturer's directions, making adjustments for temperature and humidity accordingly.

19

Coping with Building Codes

Porches are mandated by the same local, state, and national codes governing the safe design and use of all buildings; whenever one code differs from another, the most stringent one is deemed to apply. Usually, these codes do not affect the individual homeowner unless extensive renovations require application for a building permit. When this happens, and the porch is included in the scope of work, the porch becomes subject to code requirements. However, where safety is concerned, it is legally the owner's responsibility to take the initiative to prevent accidents.

The following are some of the national building codes affecting porches and suggestions for mitigating the visual impact of some of the code requirements. Different codes apply for one-, two-, and multiple-family houses and commercial buildings. Many times, the adaptive reuse of historic houses requires a more stringent application of commercial codes for public exits, which naturally involves the porch. Keep in mind that although the most stringent code applies in each case, the building inspector has some leeway in the interpretation and application of the requirements. Don't be afraid to suggest creative alternatives to improve the visual impact of code requirements.

Stairways

The stair should be protected from the accumulation of snow and ice. This means that the area of the porch roof over the stair will require a gutter. However, the building inspector may opt to allow the installation of a "cricket" to direct the water off the roof.

The width of the stair shall not be less than three feet, with the stair rail projecting no more than three and a half inches into the stairway. If the stair is less than forty-four inches, you are required to provide only one stair rail. If the stair measures more than forty-four inches but is eighty-eight inches or less, two rails are required. If, however, the stair is wider than eighty-eight inches, you may be required to install a third stair rail dividing the stairway into portions of forty-four inches or less. If this third rail detracts from the design of the stair, then a simple pipe rail, painted to match the body of the porch, should be installed.

A stair tread may vary from nine inches for one- or two-family houses to a minimum required width of eleven inches for all other building types. The riser may vary from four to seven inches in one- or two-family houses to an absolute requirement of seven inches high for all other building types. The height of the risers cannot vary more than three-eights of an inch. The tread should also project at least an inch over the edge of the closed riser.

Railings

Railings are required on all porches more than two steps above the ground. The railings must have balusters or pickets spaced so that a sphere of six inches could not pass between them. This is designed to prevent small children from falling through the railings to the ground, or getting stuck between them. Unfortunately, these things happen quite frequently, even with six-inch intervals, so it may be advisable to design intermediary inserts to decrease the spacing to four or five inches. This could be accomplished with thin horizontal or vertical slats. The smaller the slats, the less visual impact, which is to be desired.

The minimum height for a railing is forty-two inches above the finished floor. Here again, there may be some flexibility based on several factors. For instance, if the porch is only two and a half feet from the ground, the building inspector may allow the original rail to remain. If the height above the ground is greater, you may want to comply for safety purposes. It is not necessary to replace the entire railing system, however, because the building inspector frequently allows the owner to insert a simple wood or iron rail at the correct height. When you have to replace the hand rail, keep in mind that the maximum cross-sectional dimension must not exceed two and five-eighths inches. Some creative solutions to meet these requirements include using fixed flower boxes instead of installing railings or adding flower boxes secured to the top of existing railings to meet the required height.

Your particular porch restoration will be unique and the building code may have an impact on all or none of it. There are certain types of construction, however, that almost always bring the building code into play. Check with your local building department before starting work on:

- installation of awnings, whether fixed or permanent
- ramp design for public access
- French doors or windows that open onto the porch

20

Conclusion

There are many factors in repairing an old porch that require careful planning and coordination in order to save time, money, and, later remedial work. If you are reconstructing a porch removed years ago, you should check with the local building inspector to determine whether you need a building permit or variances. After work has been cleared with the local authorities, you can begin scheduling your project. This is the point at which the scope of the damage should be fully assessed. Obviously the structural work must be attended to first. Some of the secondary work, however, can be scheduled to overlap, especially if it will take time to replace an element. If, for instance, the foundation of a porch needs to be repaired but you are also planning to replace modern iron posts and rails with authentic wooden posts and rails, as well as ordering new copper gutters for the roof, you should develop a schedule that coordinates these priorities. The lead time for the gutters is four to six weeks. Replication of the rail, unless you plan to make it or find it yourself, depends on the schedule of the lumberyard. If the work is properly timed, you can be carting back suitable replacement columns from the local salvage yard just as the foundation is finished and ready to receive them. If the porch is not ready, you simply have to make provisions for storing the millwork to protect it before it is painted.

Another key aspect of repairing an old porch is the importance of saving scraps, those elements that you have determined to be unsalvageable. Before the scraps are carted off, make sure they have given you as much information as possible. A rotted cornice, for example, may provide the template and profile for the new one (make sure to allow for paint thickness). Rails, lattice, and brackets provide vital clues to the original porch design as well as to subsequent renovations. Scraps of lumber are also clues to the color history of the house. It is possible to discover whether a part of the porch is original by matching its color history, told in the paint chips, with parts of the house known to be original.

Do not forget to incorporate electrical outlets and light fixtures into your work schedule. Light fixtures should be chosen to complement the style of the porch. Again, the salvage yard may be the best place to search for fixtures. Used fixtures may need rewiring, but may be both less expensive and more authentic looking than reproductions.

A Case Study

The house shown in Fig. 167, a "before" photograph, had once been a grand residence in a major New England city. When it was purchased by new owners, they asked us how the house might have looked when it was originally built. Unfortunately, there were no existing photographs of the building when it was younger. This meant that we had to research other houses built about that time, in about the same area, with about the same amount of architectural detail. The few remaining architectural details left

Figure 167.

on the house, such as the window hoods and the floor-to-ceiling windows

Figure 168.

on the ground floor, suggested a level of craftsmanship and proportions of the house of a well-to-do homeowner. A quick survey of the surrounding area revealed little. Most of the houses in this category had either been torn down during an urban renewal project or were of a later architectural style. Finally, in the local historical society's files, we found a photograph of a similar house (Fig. 168). This second house was on the other end of town but shared many characteristics.

The last step in our quick research project was to investigate pattern books of the era. This proved to be the most helpful measure of all, providing us with several images that worked with the design and proportion of the house (Fig. 169). The historic pattern books gave us ideas for the details of the posts and a design for the doors. We also found suggestions for the window surrounds, which we combined with the remaining details on the windows to create "new" historic porch windows.

The porch apron was composed of two simple boards. It would have been nice to do something exotic, but we only had twenty-one inches in which to fit a functional porch apron. On the positive side, this short distance from the ground meant we were not faced with the difficulty or the cost of creating a railing. The sketch of the proposed "after" image shows how simple it can be to redesign a "remuddled" porch (Fig. 170).

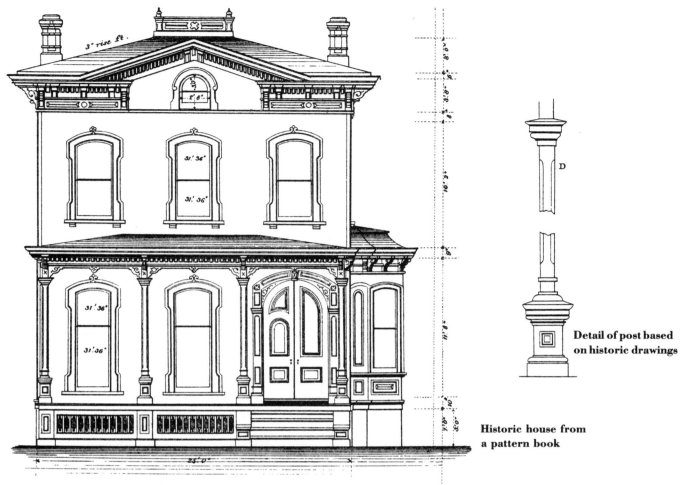

Detail of post based on historic drawings

Historic house from a pattern book

Figure 169.

Figure 170.

Sources of Supply

Many woodworking companies can provide both stock and custom reproductions for the repair of your porch. Here are some of the currently active ones. Updated information on them is available through publications such as the following: *The Old-House Journal Catalog*, updated annually, which lists hundreds of firms specializing in products for the older house and is available through The Old-House Journal Bookshop, 435 Ninth Street, Brooklyn, NY 11215 (718) 788-1700; and *Traditional Building*, a bimonthly publication, devoted to listing and evaluating products for the older buildings (back issues available), 69A Seventh Avenue, Brooklyn, NY 11217 (718) 636-0788.

Architectural Wood Columns

American Wood Column
913 Grand Street
Brooklyn, NY 11211
(212) 782-3163

Architectural Cataloguer
PO Box 8270
Galveston, TX 77553
(409) 763-4969

Boise Moulding & Lumber
116 East 44th Street
Boise, ID 83714
(208) 322-6066

Chadsworth
PO Box 53268
Atlanta, GA 30355
(404) 876-5410

Hartmann-Sanders Column Co.
4340 Bankers Circle
Atlanta, GA 30360
(800) 241-4303

Henderson, Black & Greene
PO Box 589
Troy, AL 36081
(205) 556-5000

Pagliacco Turning and Milling
PO Box 225
Woodacre, CA 94973-0225
(415) 488-4333

Remodelers & Renovators
Box 45478
Boise, ID 83711
(800) 456-2135

A. F. Schwerd Manufacturing Co.
3215 McClure Ave.
Pittsburgh, PA 15212
(412) 766-6322

Somerset Door & Column
Box 328
Somerset, PA 15501
(800) 242-7916 in PA;
(800) 242-7915

Worthington Group
PO Box 53101
Atlanta, GA 30355
(800) 872-1608

Reproductions of Historical Ornament

Anthony Wood Products
PO Box 1081
Hillsboro, TX 76645
(817) 582-7225

Classic Architectural Specialties
3223 Canton
Dallas, TX 75226
(800) 662-1221

Cumberland Woodcraft
PO Drawer 609
Carlisle, PA 17013
(717) 243-0063

Custom Millwork
PO Box 562
Berryville, VA 22611
(703) 955-4988

Custom Woodturning
4000 Telephone, Suite B13
Houston, TX 77087
(713) 641-6254

The Gazebo and Porchworks
728 9th Avenue S.W.
Puyallup, WA 98371
(206) 848-0502

Heritage Woodcraft
1230 Oakland Street
Hendersonville, NC 28739
(704) 692-8542

Mad River Woodworks
PO Box 1067
Blue Lake, CA 95525
(707) 668-5671

Mendocino Millwork
Box 669
Mendocino, CA 95460
(707) 937-4410

New England Woodturners
PO Box 7242
New Haven, CT 06519
(203) 776-1880

Pasternak's Emporium
2515 Morse at Westheimer
Houston, TX 77019
(713) 528-3808

Renovation Concepts Millwork
213 Washington Avenue N.
Minneapolis, MN 55401
(612) 333-5766

Scott Williams & Co.
310 Scott Street
Beaufort, SC 29901
(803) 525-9663

Silver Creek Mill
1335 West Highway 76
Branson, MO 65616
(417) 335-6645

Silverton Victorian Millworks
PO Box 2987
Durango, CO 81302
(303) 259-5915

Vintage Wood Works
513 South Adams
Fredericksburg, TX 78624
(512) 997-9513

Wood Factory
901 Harvard
Houston, TX 77008
(713) 863-7600

Porch Lighting

Rejuvenation House Parts Co.
901-B North Skimore
Portland, OR 97217
(503) 249-0774

Architectural Salvage

American Architectural Antiques
PO Box 1892
100 Orange Street
New Haven, CT 06508
(203) 624-1009

Antiquaria
60 Dartmouth Street
Springfield, MA 01109
(413) 781-6927

The Architectural Antiques
Warehouse
PO Box 3065, Station D
Ottawa, Ontario, Canada K1P6H6
(613) 526-1818

Architectural Antiques
121 East Sheridan
Oklahoma City, OK 73104
(405) 232-0759

Architectural Antiques, Ltd.
1321 East 2nd Street
Little Rock, AR 72202
(501) 372-1744

Architectural Antiques Exchange
715 North Second Street
Philadelphia, PA 19123
(215) 922-3669

Architectural Salvage Co-operative
909 West 3rd Street
Davenport, IA 52803
(319) 324-1556

Artefact Architectural Antiques
130 South Main Street
Doylestown, PA 18901
(215) 340-1213

Bank Architectural Antiques
1824 Felicity Street
New Orleans, LA 70113
(504) 523-2702

ByGone Era Architectural Antiques
4783 Peachtree Road
Atlanta, GA 30341
(404) 458-3016

Eifel Antiques Warehouse
571 Carroll Street
Brooklyn, NY 11215
(718) 783-4112

Fellenz Antiques—Architectural
Artifacts
439 North Euclid Avenue
St. Louis, MO 63108
(314) 367-0214

Florida Victorian Architectural
Antiques
112 Georgia Avenue
Deland, FL 32720
(904) 734-9300

Great American Salvage
34 Cooper Square
New York, NY 10003
(212) 505-0070

Other locations:
Montpelier, VT: (802) 223-7711
New Haven, CT: (203) 624-1009
Sag Harbor, NY: (516) 725-2272
Jacksonville, FL: (904) 396-8081
Middleburg, VA: (703) 687-5980

New York City Landmarks
Preservation Commission
20 Vesey Street
New York, NY 10007
(212) 553-1100

Poor Man's Paradise
Danbury—Newtown Road, Route 6
Danbury, CT 06470
(203) 748-2840

Salvage One
1524 South Sangamon Street
Chicago, IL 60608
(312) 733-0098

Stamford Housewrecking Co.
1 Barry Place
Stamford, CT 06902
(203) 324-9537

United Housewrecking
535 Hope Street
Stamford, CT 06906
(203) 348-5371

Urban Archaeology
137 Spring Street
New York, NY 10012
(212) 431-6969

Glossary

Apron The panel covering the unsightly area between the porch floor and the ground, allowing air to circulate underneath. There were two principal styles of aprons: cutwork, a board with the ventilation pattern cut with a scroll or a jigsaw, or lattice style, made up of criss-crossed wooden slats, 1″ to 1½″ x ¼″ in size.

Balusters The vertical sticks used on a porch rail, usually urn shaped with a swelling at the base or in the center.

Balustrade A continuous horizontal rail supported by the balusters. The term is Renaissance in origin and is used to describe more elaborate porch rails.

Base A molded or unmolded section under the shaft of the column.

Bracket An angled support piece placed between a vertical and a horizontal surface. Brackets may be curvilinear (made up of multiple curves cut with a scroll or jigsaw), arched (a curved stick designed to create the appearance of an arch), or Stick style, with planed-down or chamfered edges placed on an angle between the porch posts and the lintel. Brackets were designed to increase strength as well as for decoration.

Capital The molded or sculpted upper portion of a column or pilaster.

Chamfered An angle formed by flattening out or beveling the corner of a wooden porch post or bracket. This procedure is not only decorative but avoids the damage that might be caused by a sharp corner.

Classical Detail Triglyphs, metopes, fret, dentil, modillions, egg and dart, course, entablature, frieze, ornament derived from Greek and Roman architecture.

Corinthian Column A tall, slender, fluted column with the capitals decorated on all four sides with leaves derived from the acanthus plant.

Cornice The molding that covers the angle where the ceiling and wall meet.

Cresting A continuous band of ornamentation, usually metal or pierced wood, placed along the edge of the roofline.

Dentils Small, square, slightly projecting blocks used to ornament Ionic and Corinthian cornices. Taken from the Latin for "teeth."

Dentil Course A row of dentils.

Doric Column A fluted column with a plain, rounded capital.

Entablature The horizontal part of a Classical porch above the columns or pilasters. It is made up of three parts; the lowest is the *architrave*, the middle the *frieze*. The top part that projects out is called the *cornice*.

Entasis The slight bulge in a Classical column, supposedly designed to create the optical illusion of the column being straight.

Epoxy Consolidation The two-part method whereby decayed wood can be strengthened and restored.

Fenestration The arrangement of windows.

Flashing The protective material (copper or tin) used to cover the joints between two surfaces.

Fluting Vertical grooves on a Classical column.

Footings The lowest layers of material used in the foundation.

Gingerbread General term used to describe architectural ornament created by jig or scroll saw. Derived from the German term for an elaborately decorated cake.

Gothic Architecture from, or derived from, the period from A.D. 1200–1500. It featured the pointed arch and flying buttress and includes *Compound (clustered) column*, a column formed by four to five shafts joined together in a common base and capital; *quatrefoil*, a four-lobed opening, and *trefoil*, with three lobes; and *tracery*, the branching stonework at the top of a Gothic window.

Ionic Column A fluted column with a capital decorated with scroll-like spirals, called volutes.

Joists The long wooden boards placed in parallel lines across the end beams in order to support the floorboards. A typical size is 9″ to 10″ x 2½″.

Lintel A horizontal crosspiece resting on two vertical support pieces at either end that carries the weight of a beam over a window or door.

Loggia An open, columned or arched walkway set within the body of the building, rather than a projecting type of porch.

Newel or **Newel Post** A heavy post at base of a stair rail.

Palladian Eighteenth-century English and American architecture modeled after the work of the Italian architect Andrea Palladio, 1518–1580.

Pedestal The molded trim base for a column, usually the height of the rail and designed to increase the strength of the column.

Pediment The triangular shape formed by the angles of the roof in a Greek or Roman temple. Since Renaissance times, it appears over doors and windows as well, sometimes arched or broken.

Piazza Another popular Victorian name for a veranda or porch. Erroneously taken from the arched walkways around the Italian *piazza*, or square plaza.

Piers Vertical masonry supports, thicker and heavier than columns or pillars. *Battered piers* are piers that slope inward toward the top.

Pilaster A flattened portion of a column projecting slightly out from the wall. It is basically a relief with no structural function, and serves only to echo the design of the free-standing columns.

Porch An open or enclosed gallery or room attached to the outside of a building. Term is often used interchangeably with "veranda," "piazza," "loggia."

Portico A large, classically columned porch with a pedimented roof. Sometimes used to describe small, two-columned entry porches as well.

Rafters The sloping wooden beams that support the roof covering.

Soffit The underside of the cornice or any architectural part.

Spindle A small stick turned on a lathe used as part of a railing.

Trellis A lattice formed of thin wooden strips nailed together where they cross.

Tuscan Column A very plain, unfluted column with a rounded, unornamented capital and base.

Veranda A Hindustani term, adopted by the British in India, describing a long, covered porch.

Bibliography

While many other reference books and magazines exist, the following were chosen on the basis of their usefulness and availability to anyone attempting to restore a nineteenth-century or early-twentieth-century home.

Architectural Elements: The Technological Revolution. Edited by Diana S. Waite. New York: Bonanza Books, n.d.
  Replicates material from several different manufacturers, including both cast-iron and wood porch parts.

Barber, George F. *The Cottage Souvenir #2.* Watkins Glen, N.Y.: American Life Foundation and Study Institute, 1982.
  Touted as "A Repository of Artistic Cottage Architecture," Barber's book contains outrageous examples of late-nineteenth-century Eclectic design. If you are at all interested in Queen Anne–style houses, this reprint is required reading.

Benjamin, Asher. *The Architect or Practical House Carpenter.* 1830. Reprint. New York: Dover Publications, 1988.
  A reprint of the Asher Benjamin original that helped awaken American interest in the Greek Revival style.

Bicknell, A. J. *Bicknell's Village Builder & Supplement.* 1872. Reprint. Watkins Glen, N.Y.: American Life Foundation and Study Institute, 1976.
  A copy of the 1872 original featuring plans, elevations, and details for building in the Victorian Gothic and Second Empire styles.

Bicknell, A. J., and William Comstock. *Victorian Architecture.* 1873. Reprint. Watkins Glen, N.Y.: American Life Foundation and Study Institute, 1981.
  A reprint of two pattern books, one from 1873, the other from 1881, illustrating cottages and villas in mid- and late-Victorian styles.

Downing, A. J. *The Architecture of Country Houses.* 1850. Reprint. New York: Dover Publications, 1969.
  A reprint of the influential 1850 book with illustrated details of Gothic Revival and Italianate houses and porches.

Grow, Lawrence, comp. *Old House Plans.* New York: Universe Books, 1978.
  A useful overview of thirteen popular American building styles from the seventeenth to the twentieth century.

Hanson, Shirley, and Nancy Hubby. *Preserving and Maintaining the Older Home.* New York: McGraw Hill, 1983.
  Contains a well-illustrated chapter on American porch styles and maintenance problems.

Karp, Ben. *Ornamental Carpentry on Nineteenth Century American Houses.* New York: Dover Publications, 1981.

Excellent photographic details of late-nineteenth-century architectural ornament, including many porches.

Kelly, J. Frederick. *The Early Domestic Architecture of Connecticut*. 1924. Reprint. New York: Dover Publications, 1963.
> A republication of the classic 1924 study, illustrates a number of late Colonial entry porches.

Late Victorian Architectural Details. Watkins Glen, N.Y.: American Life Foundation and Study Institute, 1978.
> An exceptionally comprehensive replica of a number of late Victorian millwork catalogs illustrating close to a thousand examples of widely available details, including porch posts, rails, brackets, etc., as well as entire assemblages.

McAlester, Virginia and Lee. *A Field Guide to American Houses*. New York: Alfred A. Knopf, 1984.
> The one indispensable guide to American architecture.

Moore, Charles, and Katherine Smith, eds. *Home Sweet Home: American Domestic Vernacular Architecture*. New York: Rizzoli, 1981.
> Contains a useful chapter on the front porch.

Moss, Roger. *Century of Color: Exterior Decoration for American Buildings 1820–1920*. Watkins Glen, N.Y.: American Life Foundation and Study Institute, 1981.
> Provides insight into nineteenth- and early-twentieth-century color selection and includes two excellent color charts.

Scully, Vincent. *The Shingle Style*. New York: Braziller, 1974.
> The definitive analysis of the Shingle style.

Sinclair, Peg B. *Victorious Victorians*. New York: Holt, Rinehart and Winston, 1985.
> A heavily illustrated guide to Victorian architecture with many excellent photographs of gingerbread porches.

Sloan, Samuel. *Sloan's Victorian Buildings*. 1865. Reprint. New York: Dover Publications, 1980.
> A reprint of the famous mid-nineteenth-century pattern book, with illustrated details of Gothic and Italianate porches.

Stevens, John Calvin, and Albert Winslow Cobb. *American Domestic Architecture*. Watkins Glen, N.Y.: American Life Foundation and Study Institute, 1978.
> A replica of the book published by two Maine architects in 1889 containing over fifty plates of turn-of-the-century Colonial Revival and Shingle styles.

Victorian Architectural Details. Watkins Glen, N.Y.: The American Life Foundation and Study Institute, 1978.
> A facsimile of two popular pattern books published in 1865 and 1873 by M. F. Cummings and C. C. Miller, this volume contains over a thousand illustrations of details of houses in the fashionable Italianate and Second Empire (Mansard) styles. Porch parts are well represented, although not always detailed enough for today's carpenter to replicate.

von Holst, Herman H. *Country and Suburban Homes of the Prairie School Period*. 1913. Reprint. New York: Dover Publications, 1982.
> This unabridged replication of von Holst's 1913 publication contains photographs and plans of houses in a wide variety of popular early-twentieth-century styles, including Bungalow, Prairie, and Colonial Revival.

White Pine Series of Architectural Monographs. New York: Russel F. Whitehead, 1925.
> The original series is still available in many public libraries and is especially useful for those interested in the Colonial or twentieth-century Colonial Revival architecture.

Magazines

The Old House Journal, 435 Ninth Street, Brooklyn, NY 11215, (718) 788-1700.
> A bimonthly publication dedicated to helping the intelligent layman restore his own home.

Traditional Building, 69A Seventh Avenue, Brooklyn, NY 11217, (718) 636-0788.
> A bimonthly newsletter emphasizing product sources and technical information for both layman and professional.

Victorian Homes, 550 Seventh Street, Brooklyn, NY 11215, (718) 499-5789.
> Also designed to assist the layman, with attractive photos and decoration advice.

Illustration Sources

Frontispiece: "A Reminiscence of White Sulphur Springs," *Harper's Weekly*, 1879.

Figure 1: The Metropolitan Museum of Art *Bulletin*. Spring 1973.

Figure 2: *Detail, Cottage and Constructive Architecture* by A. J. Bicknell (New York, 1873), plate 48.

Figure 3: *American Architect and Building News*, August 27, 1881.

Figure 4: Courtesy of the Library of Congress.

Figure 5: Deborah Berke, Berke and McWorther, Architects, New York; Steven Brooke, photographer.

Figure 6: Bernard Schoenbaum, © 1987, The New Yorker Magazine, Inc.

Figure 7: *History of the Connecticut Valley in Mass.*, by Louis Everts, Volume II (Philadelphia, 1879).

Figure 8: Engraving by Johann Theodor DeBry, c.1623.

Figure 9: 144 Olive Street, New Haven, Connecticut; Historic Neighborhood Preservation Program, Inc., Collection.

Figure 10: Courtesy of Drayton Hall, Charleston, South Carolina, a National Trust for Historic Preservation property.

Figure 11: *The Four Books of Architecture* by Andrea Palladio, Book II, plate XL (1570; reprint, New York: Dover Publications, 1965, from the 1738 English edition).

Figure 12: *Early Illustrations & Views of American Architecture* by Edmund V. Gillon, Jr. (New York: Dover Publications, 1971).

Figure 13: Courtesy of Boscobel Restoration, Garrison, New York.

Figure 14: Courtesy of the Library of Congress.

Figure 15: Louisiana Division of Historic Preservation; Patricia L. Duncan, photographer.

Figure 16: *Hutchinson and Wickersham Catalog* (New York, 1857).

Figure 17: Courtesy of the Library of Congress.

Figure 18: Historic Neighborhood Preservation Program, Inc., Collection.

Figure 19: *Early Illustrations & Views of American Architecture* by Edmund V. Gillon, Jr. (New York: Dover Publications, 1971).

Figure 20: The Shadows-on-the-Teche, New Iberia, Louisiana, a National Trust for Historic Preservation property.

Figures 21, 22, and 23: Courtesy of the Library of Congress.

Figure 24: *Picturesque Stamford 1641–1892* by Edward T. W. Gillespie (Stamford, Conn.: Gillespie Brothers, 1892).

Figure 25: *Home Library of Universal Knowledge* (Chicago: R. S. Peale, 1889).

Figure 26: *The Domestic Architect* by Oliver P. Smith (Buffalo, N.Y.: Phinney & Co., 1854), plate XXVII.

Figure 27: *Home from the Brook/The Lucky Fishermen*, Currier and Ives, 1867.

Figure 28: Courtesy of Lyndhurst, Tarrytown, New York, a National Trust for Historic Preservation property.

Figure 29: Keith Daniello, photographer.

Figures 30 and 31: *The Domestic Architect* by Oliver P. Smith (Buffalo, N.Y.: Phinney & Co., 1854).

Figure 32: Alison Clausi, photographer.

Figure 33: Courtesy of the Library of Congress.

Figure 34: *Early Illustrations & Views of American Architecture* by Edmund V. Gillon, Jr. (New York: Dover Publications, 1971).

Figure 35: Historic Neighborhood Preservation Program, Inc., Collection.

Figure 36: Louisiana Division of Historic Preservation.

Figure 37: *Architectural Designs* by John Riddell, 1861.

Figure 38: Keith Daniello, photographer.

Figure 39: Courtesy of the Library of Congress.

Figure 40: Historic Neighborhood Preservation Program, Inc., Collection.

Figure 41: *Universal Molding Book* (W. L. Churchill, 1878).

Figure 42: Keith Daniello, photographer.

Figure 43: *Universal Molding Book* (W. L. Churchill, 1878).

Figure 44: Keith Daniello, photographer.

Figure 45: Historic Neighborhood Preservation Program, Inc., Collection.

Figure 46: University of Connecticut, Waterbury campus.

Figure 47: *Universal Molding Book* (W. L. Churchill, 1878).

Figure 48: Keith Daniello, photographer.

Figure 49: *Bicknell's Village Builder, and Supplement* (New York: A. J. Bicknell & Co., 1872).

Figure 50: Historic Neighborhood Preservation Program, Inc., Collection.

Figures 51 and 52: *Early Illustrations & Views of American Architecture* by Edmund V. Gillon, Jr. (New York: Dover Publications, 1971).

Figure 53: Keith Daniello, photographer.

Figure 54: *Frank Leslie's Illustrated News*, 1876.

Figure 55: *Indoors and Out*, May 1907.

Figure 56: Historic Neighborhood Preservation Program, Inc., Collection.

Figures 57 and 58: *Universal Molding Book* (W. L. Churchill, 1878).

Figure 59: Historic Neighborhood Preservation Program, Inc., Collection.

Figure 60: "Design for a City House" by C. D. Marvin, architect, New York, in *Architecture and Building*, 1891.

Figure 61: Keith Daniello, photographer.

Figure 62: *Henry Hudson Richardson and His Works* by Marina G. Van Renssalaer (New York: Houghton, Mifflin and Company, 1888).

Figure 63: *Picturesque Stamford 1641–1892* by Edward

T. W. Gillespie (Stamford, Conn.: Gillespie Brothers, 1892).

Figure 64: *Combined Book of Sash, Doors, Blinds, Mouldings, Etc.* (Chicago: Rand, McNally & Co., 1898).

Figure 65: Historic Neighborhood Preservation Program, Inc., Collection.

Figure 66: Don Piper, photographer.

Figures 67 and 68: *Combined Book of Sash, Doors, Blinds, Mouldings, Etc.* (Chicago: Rand, McNally & Co., 1898).

Figure 69: *Modern Dwellings in Town and Country* by H. Hudson Holly (New York: Harper and Brothers, 1878).

Figure 70: *American Architect*, 1879.

Figures 71 and 72: *Artistic Country Seats; Types of Recent American Villas and Cottage Architecture with Instances of Country Club-Houses* by George William Sheldon (New York, 1886–1887).

Figure 73: Historic Neighborhood Preservation Program, Inc., Collection.

Figures 74 and 75: Keith Daniello, photographer.

Figure 76: Historic Neighborhood Preservation Program, Inc., Collection.

Figure 77: *Appleton's Home Book: Building a Home* by A. F. Oakey (New York: D. Appleton & Co., 1881).

Figure 78: *Bungalows* by Henry H. Saylor (New York: McBride, Nast & Company, 1913).

Figure 79: *Radford's Portfolio of Plans* by Wm. Radford (New York: The Radford Architectural Company, 1909).

Figure 80: *Modern American Homes* (Chicago: American Technical Society, 1913).

Figure 81: *The Craftsman* 15, no. 6 (March 1909).

Figure 82: Alison Clausi, photographer.

Figures 83 and 84: Donald Piper, photographer.

Figure 85: House in Glenwood Landing, Long Island, by Schell Lewis, architect, in *The Architect*, November 1927.

Figure 86: Historic Neighborhood Preservation Program, Inc., Collection.

Figure 87: *Radford's Portfolio of Plans* by Wm. Radford (New York: The Radford Architectural Company, 1909).

Figure 88: Historic Neighborhood Preservation Program, Inc., Collection.

Figure 89: House in Scarsdale, New York, by Eugene J. Lang, architect, in *The Architect*, April 1928.

Figure 90: House in Pittsfield, Massachusetts, by Charles S. Keefe, architect, in *The Architect*, November 1930.

Figure 91: Courtesy of Lyndhurst, Tarrytown, New York, a National Trust for Historic Preservation property.

Figure 92: *Indoors and Out*, November 1907.

Figure 93: *House & Garden*, January 1929.

Figure 94: *Villas and Cottages* by Calvert Vaux, revised edition (New York, 1863).

Figure 95: Don Piper, photographer.

Figure 96: House in Mill Neck, Long Island, by Hart & Shape, architects, in *The Architect*, June 1928.

Figure 97: *Small Homes of Distinction* by Robert T. Jones (New York: Harper & Bros., 1929).

Figure 98: House in Pasadena, California, by Reginald D. Johnson, architect, in *The Architect*, April 1930.

Figure 99: *Small Homes of Distinction* by Robert T. Jones (New York: Harper & Bros., 1929).

Figure 100: Don Piper, photographer.

Figure 101: *Indoors and Out*, November 1907.

Figure 102: Historic Neighborhood Preservation Program, Inc., Collection.

Figure 103: *Modern American Homes* (Chicago: American Technical Society, 1912).

Figure 104: *Radford's Portfolio of Plans* by Wm. Radford (New York: The Radford Architectural Company, 1909).

Figure 105: *The Horticulturalist* by A. J. Downing, 1846.

Figures 106 and 107: Historic Neighborhood Preservation Program, Inc., Collection.

Figure 108: *Picturesque Stamford 1641–1892* by Edward T. W. Gillespie (Stamford, Conn.: Gillespie Brothers, 1892).

Figure 109: Keith Daniello, photographer.

Figure 110: House in Black Rock, Connecticut, courtesy of Fairfield Historical Society.

Figure 114: Ellen Meagher.

Figure 115: Alison Clausi, photographer.

Figures 118 and 119: Ellen Meagher.

Figure 120: National Association of Homebuilders.

Figures 122, 125, 127, 128, 129, and 130: Ellen Meagher.

Figure 134: *Bicknell's Village Builder, and Supplement* (New York: A. J. Bicknell & Co., 1872).

Figure 136: Keith Daniello, photographer.

Figure 137: *Bicknell's Village Builder, and Supplement* (New York: A. J. Bicknell & Co., 1872).

Figure 149: Alison Clausi, photographer.

Figure 150: Historic Neighborhood Preservation Program, Inc., Collection.

Figures 152 and 153: Keith Daniello, photographer.

Figure 154: Ellen Meagher and Alison Clausi, photographers.

Figures 155 and 156: Alison Clausi, photographer.

Figures 157 and 161: Ellen Meagher.

Figure 164: Stephen Smith home in South Field Point, Connecticut, *c.* 1888, courtesy of Stamford Historical Society.

Figures 165 and 166: Keith Daniello, photographer.

Figures 167 and 168: Historic Neighborhood Preservation Program, Inc., Collection.

Figure 169: *Bicknell's Village Builder, and Supplement* (New York: A. J. Bicknell & Co., 1872).

Index